EASTERN FRONT FROM PRIMARY SOURCES

WINTER WARFARE ON THE RUSSIAN FRONT

EDITED AND INTRODUCED BY BOB CARRUTHERS

CODA
BOOKS LTD

This edition published in Great Britain in 2012 by
Coda Books Ltd, The Barn, Cutlers Farm Business Centre, Edstone,
Wootton Wawen, Henley in Arden, Warwickshire, B95 6DJ
www.codabooks.com

Copyright © 2012 Coda Books Ltd

All rights reserved. No part of this publication may be reproduced or
transmitted in any form or by any means, electronic or mechanical,
including photocopy, recording, or any information storage and retrieval
system, without permission in writing from the publisher.

A CIP catalogue record for this book is available from the British Library
ISBN 978 1 78158 168 1

CONTENTS

Introduction 5
Effects of Climate on Combat in European Russia 7
   Preface 7
   Introduction 9
   WINTER 10
      General 10
      Snow 16
      German Tactics 19
      Russian Tactics 23
      Clothing, Equipment, Rations 26
      Transportation and Troop Movements 28
      Health and Morale 32
      Air Operations 33
   NORTH OF THE ARCTIC CIRCLE 35
      General 35
      Clothing, Equipment, Rations 40
      Transportation and Troop Movements 45
      Health and Morale 48
      Air Operations 50
   Conclusions 53

Warfare in the Far North 54
   Preface 54
   The Climate 55
   The Terrain 60
   Organization and Tactics 71
   Prospects 82

Small Unit Actions during the Russian Campaign:
Company G 86

The Struggle for Shelter (December 1941) 115

Seesaw Battle in Subzero Temperatures (January 1942) 121

German Raid on a Russian Strong Point in Northern Finland (February 1944) 124

Morale during winter 133

Finnish Tactics - Small Units 137

Combat in High Mountains, Snow, and Extreme Cold 146

Winter Flying Problems 153

Sleds for Winter Warfare 161

German Ambulance Sled 164

Snow camouflage 165

German winter field fortifications and the use of ice-concrete 167

Winter Fighting in Russia 175

Notes on Winter Use of Infantry Weapons 187

Russian Tank Camouflage in Winter 193

Engineer Practices in Winter 200

ABOUT CODA BOOKS 206

INTRODUCTION

This book forms part of the series entitled 'Eastern Front from Primary Sources.' The aim is to provide the reader with a varied range of materials drawn from original writings covering the strategic, operational and tactical aspects of the battles of Hitler's war in the east. The concept behind the series is to provide the well-read and knowledgeable reader with an interesting compilation of related primary sources which together build a picture of a particular aspect of the titanic struggle on the Eastern Front.

I am pleased to report that the series has been well received and it is a pleasure to be able to bring original primary sources to the attention of an interested readership. I particularly enjoy discovering new primary sources, and I am pleased to be able to present them unadorned and unvarnished to a sophisticated audience. The sources speak for themselves and the readership I strive to serve is the increasingly well informed community of reader/historians which needs no editorial lead and can draw its own conclusions. I am well aware that our community is constantly striving to discover new nuggets of information, and I trust that with this volume I have managed to stimulate fresh enthusiasm and that some of these articles will provoke readers to research further down these lines of investigation, and perhaps cause established views to be challenged once more. I am aware at all times in compiling these materials that our relentless pursuit of more and better historical information is at the core our common passion. I trust that this selection will contribute to that search and will help all of us to better comprehend and understand the bewildering events of the last century.

The centre piece of this volume is the often overlooked US Army study 'Effects of Climate on Combat in European Russia', a series of post war debriefs written by Generaloberst Erhard

Rauss, Commander, 4th and 3rd Panzer Armies, for the US Army Historical department. It is highly illuminating and gives a good insight into the struggles of simply surviving the bitter winter conditions, let alone fighting. There is also a section on combat in the Arctic Circle with the Finnish Army.

In order to produce an interesting compilation giving a flavour of events at the tactical level I have returned once more to the US Intelligence series of pamphlets, which contain an intriguing series of contemporary articles on weapons and tactics. I find this series of pamphlets particularly fascinating as they are written in the present tense and, as such, provide us with a sense of what was happening at the face of battle as events unfolded.

Thank you very much for buying this volume, I hope you find something new and interesting in these pages and I sincerely hope it earns its place in your library.

Bob Carruthers
Edinburgh 2012.

EFFECTS OF CLIMATE ON COMBAT IN EUROPEAN RUSSIA

By Generaloberst Erhard Rauss Commander, 4th and 3rd Panzer Armies

Preface

'Effects of Climate in Combat in European Russia' was prepared by a committee of former German generals and general staff officers under the supervision of the Historical Division, EUCOM. The material, based on the personal experiences of the principal author and his associates, was written largely from memory, with some assistance from diaries, earlier studies, and documents. All the German officers involved had extensive experience on the Eastern Front during the period 1941-45. The principal author, for example, commanded in succession a panzer division, a panzer army, and an army group.

The reader is reminded that publications in the GERMAN REPORT SERIES were written by Germans from the German point of view. As in Department of the Army Pamphlet No. 20-230, Russian Combat Methods in World War II, and Department of the Army Pamphlet No. 20-290, Terrain Factors in the Russian Campaign, the 'Introduction' and 'Conclusions' to this study present the views of the German author without interpretation by American personnel. Minor changes in form and in chapter titles have been made to obtain greater clarity. However, passages which may reflect the authors' prejudices and defects, whatever they may be, have not been changed, and find the same expression in the following translation as they do in the original German.

Department of the Army February 1952

General reference map

Introduction

The purpose of this study is to describe the climatic conditions encountered by the German armed forces during four years of struggle in European Russia. To this end the climate of the various regions is described together with its effects on men and equipment, combat and supply. The first three sections are concerned with European Russia south of the Arctic Circle, the last treats of European Russia north of the Arctic Circle. The study emphasizes the lessons learned and improvisations employed to surmount difficult situations.

A Western European army fighting in Russia is faced with conditions entirely different from those to which it is accustomed, conditions rooted in the peculiarities of Russia and its people. The most unusual characteristic of the country is the climate, which affects terrain and vegetation and determines living conditions in general. The climate leaves its mark upon the Russian and his land, and he who steps for the first time on Russian soil is immediately conscious of the new, the strange, the primitive.

The German soldier who crossed into Russian territory felt that he entered a different world, where he was opposed not only by the forces of the enemy but also by the forces of nature. Nature is the ally of the Russian Army, and the struggle against this alliance was a severe test for the Wehrmacht, exacting great sacrifices. To conquer the raging elements of nature was the more difficult because their fury and effect were not fully recognized by the Germans, who were neither trained nor equipped to withstand them. The German command had been under the impression that the Red Army could be destroyed west of the Dnepr, and that there would be no need for conducting operations in cold, snow, and mud.

WINTER
GENERAL

Winter in most parts of European Russia south of the Arctic Circle sets in suddenly and lasts five to six months. The period of clear weather which follows the autumn muddy season lasts at most one month, too short a time for extensive military operations. Cold ice and snow may hinder operations as early as December, especially in the northern parts of the country.

Snowfall varies greatly in European Russia. It is greater in the northern and central regions than in the south. Along the lower Don and Donets, in the winter of 1942-43, the first snow fell in mid-December and did not affect mobility during the entire winter. The same winter saw more than eighteen inches of snow on the middle course of these rivers and in the Kharkov area. Snow depths of three to four feet are common in the north, where wheeled vehicles can move only on cleared roads, and huge snowdrifts build up in valleys and hollows. Here horse-mounted and dismounted troops move with difficulty except on roads, and trail breakers must be used for crosscountry marches. In deep-snow country even tanks and other tracked vehicles are restricted to plowed roads.

In the Baltic and Leningrad regions the snow cover varies greatly from year to year. Leningrad and its vicinity, for example, may have as much as twenty-eight inches of snow in severe winters, while in mild winters there may be less than two inches. Water courses to the south of Leningrad often freeze over by mid-November, and temperatures there may fall as low as -40° F. Even during mild winters the mercury will drop to -20° F.

In central European Russia, the Smolensk-Vitebsk area has noon temperatures below freezing even during average winters. The Pripyat Marshes usually freeze over in winter, and only during exceptionally mild winters, or in case of an early snow cover, will large patches of the Pripyat remain unfrozen and impassable.

The winter of the southern steppes, longer and colder than that of Central Europe, differs little from the winter of central and northern Russia south of the Arctic Circle. In the Black Sea region, where two thirds of the annual precipitation occurs between September and March, the climate is of the Mediterranean type.

The winter of 1941-42 was most severe in European Russia. In the area northwest of Moscow the mean temperature during January 1942 was -32°F, and the 26th of the month in the same area saw the lowest recorded temperature of the entire Russian campaign: -63°F. The southern part of European Russia, too, had record low temperatures during the first winter, with readings ranging from -22° to -40° F., compared with temperatures of 14° to -40° F., in the same area during The obliteration of landmarks in snow-covered terrain makes orientation difficult. Russian villages are hard to identify from a distance, and often a church built on high ground or a church tower is the only visible sign of an inhabited place. If neither is present, woods filled with screeching birds usually indicate that a village is near by. The Russian peasant stores his winter supplies in advance and digs in to spend the winter completely cut off from the outside world.

Cold reduces the efficiency of men and weapons. At the beginning of December 1941, 6th Panzer Division was but 9 miles from Moscow and 15 miles from the Kremlin when a sudden drop in temperature to -30° F., coupled with a surprise attack by Siberian troops, smashed its drive on the capital. Paralyzed by cold, the German troops could not aim their rifle fire, and bolt mechanisms jammed or strikers shattered in the bitter winter weather. Machine guns became encrusted with ice, recoil liquid froze in guns, ammunition supply failed. Mortar shells detonated in deep snow with a hollow, harmless thud, and mines were no longer reliable. Only one German tank in ten had survived the autumn muddy season, and those still available could not move through the snow because of their narrow tracks.

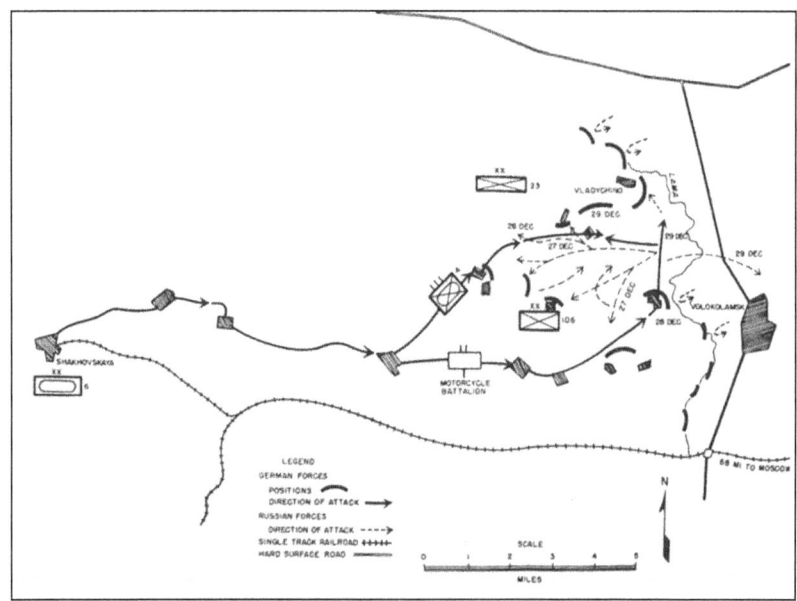

MAP 2. Counterattack by 6th Panzer Division near Volokolamsk 28-29 December 1941.

At first the Russian attack was slowed with hand grenades, but after a few days the German prepared positions in villages and farmhouses were surrounded or penetrated.

The Germans held out to the northwest of Moscow until 5 December, and on the next day the first retreat order of the war was given. In the months of the offensive, German battalions and companies had dwindled to a handful of men. The Russian mud and winter had wrought havoc upon their weapons and equipment. Leadership and bravery could not compensate for the lowered fire power of the German divisions. The numerical superiority of the Russians, aided by climatic conditions, saved Moscow and turned the tide of battle. Hitler neither expected nor planned for a winter war.

By mid-December, when the first phase of the German withdrawal ended, 6th Panzer Division was located in Shakhovskaya to refit and receive reinforcements. (Map 2) On Christmas Eve the 4th Armored Infantry Regiment, which had received replacements, was alerted to counterattack Russian forces that had broken through German positions on the Lama River west of Volokolamsk, in the sector of the 106th Infantry Division.

On 26 December the regiment moved out in a snowstorm over roads already covered with deep drifts. The German troops were inadequately clothed for the Russian winter, and in every village lengthy warming halts were necessary. Two days were needed to cover the twelve miles to the line of departure.

After a meal and a night's rest, 4th Armored Infantry Regiment attacked on 28 December together with German elements already in the area. Well supported by artillery and heavy weapons, the regiment advanced throughout the day, and in the evening made contact with the 23d Infantry Division to the north, thus closing the gap. Some shelter was found in nearby villages and farmhouses. Strong security detachments were posted, and relieved every half hour because of the extreme cold.

The plan for 29 December was to regain the former German positions on the Lama by envelopment of the Russian forces that had broken through. The regiment attacked eastward while the motorcycle battalion of the 6th Panzer Division, south of the main body, advanced northward toward Vladychino. By noon the enemy break-through force was surrounded.

Night temperatures dropped to between -30° and -40° F., and no shelter was available to the German troops. The near-by villages were destroyed and the entrenchments of the old German positions on the Lama were buried deep in snow. To remain exposed would have meant certain death to the troops who lacked adequate winter clothing, and withdrawal to a distant village was ordered.

When the Russians observed that the encirclement had been abandoned, they concentrated for a new break-through which eventually forced a withdrawal of the entire German front in the area. Success had turned to failure because the Germans were not equipped to withstand extreme cold.

Periods of moderate cold alternating with thaw are

particularly dangerous. At the end of March 1942, in the Lake Ladoga region, noon temperatures rose to 41° F., followed by a sharp fall of the mercury at night. Boots, socks, and trousers that had become wet during the day stiffened with the night cold and froze toes and feet. Serious frost injuries developed when troops overheated from combat were forced to spend the night in snow pits or windswept open fields, especially when the fatigued men took even the shortest of naps. A German company that spent a day during a thaw entrenching itself lost sixty-five of its ninety-three men as a result of a sudden severe cold wave at night.

Frostbite casualties among German troops were heavy during the first year of the war. At the beginning of December 1941, Fourth Army failed in an attempt to penetrate the outer defenses of Moscow because the Russians were able to use the rail net around the city to bring up strong forces. On the morning of 4 December, after three days of heavy losses, army fell back to its positions of 1 December to avoid further casualties.

On the same day, as the weather turned bitter cold, the Russians attacked, and by 20 December the entire army front was heavily engaged. A radio message intercepted at the time revealed that the Russian drive was an all-out effort to knock the Germans out of the war. Later information that the Russians had deployed 30 infantry divisions, 33 infantry brigades, 6 armored brigades, and 3 cavalry divisions on the Moscow front left no doubt as to their intent.

By 5 January, when temperatures had risen somewhat, Fourth Army counted 2,000 frostbite casualties and half as many from enemy action. At this point Hitler gave permission to pull back the army left wing in the face of a Russian envelopment, and the withdrawal was completed according to plan. There was no let-up in the battle, however, and German casualties from all causes continued to mount. A snowstorm which, since the 5th, had added to the German difficulties, stopped on the 10th, and clear cold weather with temperatures down to $-13°$ F. followed. Here and there, supplies were moved up during quiet periods, but even then at great cost in lives and equipment.

The Germans fell back steadily and in March heavy snowfalls hampered the withdrawal as the Russian offensive continued. On 18 April, the first warm, sunny day of spring, the Russian attacks ceased. Fourth Army suffered 96,535 casualties between 1 January and 31 March 1942, of which 14,236 were frostbite cases.

Frostbite was frequent among drivers and troops who were moved long distances in open trucks. So long as suitable clothing was not available, constant indoctrination in cold-weather precautions was necessary. Frequent halts were made so men could warm themselves by exercise. Front-line troops became indifferent in extreme cold; under constant enemy pressure they became mentally numbed. Medical officers and commanders of all ranks had to make certain that soldiers changed socks frequently, and that they did not wait until swollen feet made it impossible to take off boots.

Some chemical heat packets were issued, but they protected only small areas of the body for short periods. Regular use of the sauna, a steam bath, was helpful in preventing illnesses caused by cold and exposure, but such baths were not always available.

The Russians, too, suffered from the extreme cold when forced to remain out in the open. Their supplies did not keep up with them, and they became weak and exhausted. Consequently, they always made a great effort to capture villages for overnight shelter. For example, in the winter of 1941-42, north of Rzhev, the Russians unsuccessfully attempted to drive German forces out of a village and were forced to spend the night in the open. Cut off from supplies and stiff with cold, the Russians were so weakened by their ordeal that they were unable to hinder a withdrawal of German troops, including two batteries, from north of the village, even though the Germans passed within 100 yards of the Russian forces.

Snow

A war of movement is difficult in deep snow. Foot marches in twenty inches of snow are slow; in depths of more than twenty inches they are exhausting. When snow was not too deep, the Germans used details, in shifts, to tramp down snow trails. Ski troops were also used as trail breakers. The Russians used T34 tanks to pack down snow; the tracks used on German tanks during the first year of the war were too narrow for this purpose.

Movements on foot or with wheeled vehicles are impossible in snow depths above forty inches. Snow crust is sometimes strong enough to bear the weight of small groups. Hard-frozen snow, however, can be used only for night movement, because the approach of troops over a snow crust can be heard at a great distance. Snow in bushland, draws, and ditches will not support much weight.

I. Infantry

A normal infantry attack cannot be made in deep snow. Advancing by bounds is out of the question, because every movement must be made in the open, exposed to enemy fire. If infantry attacks had to be made, the Germans always sought areas where the snow was less deep. If such areas could not be found, the infantry had to work its way forward under cover of darkness, digging as it went, or following a beaten path against the flank and rear of the enemy.

Without adequate snow removal equipment, infantry movement during or after a snowstorm is difficult. In December 1942, for example, the defeat of Italian forces in the Voronezh area made it imperative that this sector of the front be reinforced. A German infantry division near Siniye Lipyagi was made available and ordered to march the fifty-five miles south to the endangered area. The march was to be made through the rear areas of several German divisions which were to assist the advancing unit by furnishing rations and quarters, and the movement was expected to take three days.

The division set out in the first flurries of what proved to be a twelve-day blizzard. The march route was over lateral roads not used for logistical support, and consequently not cleared of snow. It was just at this time that the desperate German attempt to relieve Stalingrad required all available snowplows. Instead of the expected three days the march required fifteen. A command decision to make motorized snow-clearing equipment available would have aided the movement considerably. Such equipment, always scarce in the German Army, was controlled at army or army group level.

II. Artillery

Artillery was moved on existing roads, and if no roads were available, new tracks were shoveled. In deep snow it was often impossible for the infantry to take full advantage of artillery preparation, because it could not move forward fast enough. Such an instance occurred at Gaytolovo (a few miles south of Lake Ladoga) on 21 December 1941. The German infantry attacked at 0900 after a thorough artillery preparation. It took so long for the riflemen to reach the Russian positions that enemy bunkers went into action again, and the assault was delayed. By 1500, when the infantry had penetrated at several points, a withdrawal order was given. The troops would have frozen to death if they had spent the night in the open.

The effectiveness of artillery projectiles, particularly those of small caliber, and of mortar ammunition, was seriously hampered by deep snow. Snow dampened and reduced lateral fragmentation of artillery shells, and almost completely smothered mortar fire and hand grenades. Heavy artillery weapons, such as the German 210-mm. mortar, remained highly effective. Because of the cushioning effect of snow, mines often failed to detonate when stepped on or even when driven over by tanks. To keep detonators effective in extremely cold weather, gun crews often carried them in their pockets.

Registration fire with aerial observation and with flash and sound was hampered because the snow swallowed projectiles and bursts. Artillery map firing was impeded by a vast difference between meteorological conditions in Russia and in Central Europe, and the resultant range dispersion. Metro corrections of German observation battalions were computed according to Central European standards, resulting in less accurate fire. Checking air observation by sound and flash ranging, and checking sound ranging by flash ranging and vice versa, disclosed deviations caused by climatic factors whose ultimate causes were never fully determined. The services of qualified meteorological technicians would have been useful.

By placing fire control and radio equipment in improvised wooden containers padded with blankets it was possible to protect them against frost damage and shock. Russian peasant sleighs with built-in boxes were often used for transporting radio equipment.

III. Armored Forces

The principal shortcoming of German tanks was the narrow width of their tracks. Tanks sank deep into the snow, and because of their limited ground clearance, ultimately became stuck. Russian tanks, particularly the T34, KV1, and KV2, were able to drive through deep snow because of their good ground clearance and wide tracks, and therein lay their special effectiveness in winter warfare. After the first winter of the war, Germans started to use wide, removable tracks. These solved the problem of snow mobility, but tanks so equipped could not be moved on German railroad cars and were too wide to cross the standard German military bridge. Russian wide tank tracks were factory equipment; the broad gauge of Russian railroads with their correspondingly wide flat cars eliminated the transportation problem.

In December 1942 a German armored division, diverted from the abortive relief thrust on Stalingrad to consolidate an extremely critical situation on the Chir River front, was delayed twelve hours because the snow tracks of its tanks were too wide for a military bridge over the Don. The tracks of more than 150 tanks and assault guns had to be removed in total darkness and remounted on the far shore.

German Tactics

Unless forced by circumstances to do so, the Germans did not launch offensives in midwinter. During local attacks communication trenches or tunnels for infantry could be dug through snow with considerable speed. While such trenches offered effective concealment if skillfully sited and camouflaged, they were practically useless for protection. Whenever artillery support was needed snow had to be cleared from firing positions and ammunition storage areas.

For individual movement through snow, skis are best. Large ski units are relatively ineffective since heavy weapons cannot be carried or supplied. The Germans did not use ski troops in units above battalion size, while the Russians used such troops up to brigade strength. Skis are a hindrance in combat; they have to be removed before going into action, and often become lost.

Ski troops are effective for reconnaissance missions. For example, in March 1942, a ski patrol of 20 volunteers from the reconnaissance battalion of 6th Panzer Division infiltrated 15 miles into enemy territory, captured 3 prisoners, and gained much valuable information. Russian civilians living in the area where the reconnaissance was made, who had been well treated by Germans billeted in their villages at an earlier date, were of great assistance. Local guides led the patrol around enemy and partisan strongholds, and provided shelter in farmhouses. The mission took four days.

With the onset of the Russian winter adequate shelter is a necessity in tactical operations. His intrenching tools useless in frozen ground, the German soldier could only cower in a snow hole and wait until a dugout or similar shelter was blasted out of the frost-bound soil. Blasted shelters were usually pitch dark, and the small, open fires used for heating filled every crevice with smudge and smoke. For above-ground shelter, the Finnish-type round tent proved highly serviceable. Troops were trained to construct igloos, but this type of shelter never became popular. Native log houses in the forests of the northern and central regions of European Russia are excellent heat retainers and are highly resistant to concussion.

When German troops were attacking Tikhvin in the winter of 1941, cold set in suddenly. Lacking winter clothing and adequate shelter, the Germans suffered more casualties from cold than from enemy fire, and the attack had to be halted as the more warmly dressed and better-equipped Russians gained the initiative. The German troops were withdrawn to avoid further weather casualties.

The defender has a definite advantage in winter because, as a rule, his positions cannot be seen in snow except at very close range. He is able to keep his forces under cover and wait until the moment that fire can be used most effectively. The attacker, on the other hand, is impeded in his movements and is easily detected, even in camouflage clothing. The principal weapon of the defender is the machine gun. Its performance is not diminished by snow, in which mortars and light artillery lose most of their effectiveness.

When defensive positions were not occupied until winter, the Germans found it impossible to build shelters and emplacements in hard frozen ground. Machine guns and rifles had to be placed on a snow parapet that had been built up and packed hard. If well constructed, and water poured over it to form an ice coating, the parapet offered some protection against enemy fire.

Where organized positions are established before snowfall, parapets must be increased in height as the snow level rises, and care taken to keep trenches and approaches free of snow at all times. Trenches and dugouts provide better cover in winter than

A motorcade with white camouflage in the snow, Russia, October 1941

in other seasons. Snow-covered obstacles remain effective until covered by a snow crust that will bear a man's weight. Barriers against ski troops are effective only as long as they project above the snow. Obstacles must be removed when snow begins to melt, or they will obstruct visibility and fields of fire.

When swamps freeze over, the defender is suddenly faced with a situation changed to his disadvantage. German divisions that fought defensive actions when swamps were impassable barriers were at a great disadvantage against the same enemy, in the same location, when swamps froze over. The increased frontage created by the frozen swamp could be defended only by employing additional artillery and much greater quantities of all types of ammunition. Similarly, the winter freeze-up is disadvantageous to a weak defender behind a water barrier. The freeze turns rivers into routes of approach toward the defensive positions.

Since the Russians often penetrated artillery firing positions, the Germans trained artillerymen in infantry close-combat tactics. Because snow sometimes makes it impossible to evacuate guns, artillery crews were trained in demolition of field pieces.

The Russian, winter covers roads, countryside, and vehicles with a crippling coat of ice and, when sand is not available, entire columns are forced to halt. Icy roads can rob an offensive of surprise or be fatal to a withdrawal. Ice conditions prevail every winter in all parts of Russia. During the German withdrawal from the Moscow area in the winter of 1941-42, ice hindered the entire operation. A few days before the order to retreat from the suburbs of Moscow, 6th Panzer Division, by building a defense around its last five tanks, held off an attack by Siberian troops who presented prime targets in their brown uniforms as they trudged forward in deep snow. This local success facilitated the disengagement of the division and provided time for the destruction of its last 88-mm. antiaircraft guns, necessary because no prime movers were available. Twenty-five prime movers were lost in the autumn mud of 1941, and seven had fallen victim to winter cold and snow. The withdrawal proceeded according to plan on the first day but the next day, moving over hilly terrain, vehicles skidded on icy roads, and trucks which had been abandoned during the preceding muddy season blocked the roads, adding to the difficulties.

Fearful that the pursuing Russians would overtake and destroy the rear guard if time were spent in extricating each vehicle, the Germans loaded as much materiel as possible on trucks still serviceable and put the remaining equipment to the torch. The rear guard was reinforced, and the withdrawal continued with brief delaying actions based on villages. Inhabited places were vital to the Germans, who lacked winter clothing, and attractive, too, to the Russians who preferred permanent-type shelter. The retreat became a race from village to village.

In a few days the Germans reached Klin, northwest of Moscow, which could not be used to house the division overnight, as the city was on the main route of other divisions streaming west. However, a large quantity of explosives were found in Klin and were used to blast temporary shelters in the ground outside the city. Attempts to obtain dirt from the blasted shelters for sanding roads were useless because the explosions loosed great chunks of solidly frozen earth which could not be pulverized. The division held before Klin for one day, and then completed its withdrawal across the four-lane Smolensk-Moscow highway.

Russian air activity during the withdrawal was ineffective, because it was limited to scattered sorties of a few planes which strafed columns or dropped small fragmentation bombs. During air alerts the Germans burrowed in the snow at least 100 yards from the road. Some casualties were caused by delayed-action bombs when men failed to remain down long enough after the missiles were dropped. If the Russians had used strong bomber forces, the results would have been disastrous. In contrast to the losses from enemy air, German casualties due to cold weather and insufficient clothing were heavy. The numerically superior enemy did not succeed in enveloping and annihilating the German rear guard, because he could not employ his heavy weapons in a frontal attack in deep snow without suffering heavy losses. Successful envelopment was difficult for the Russians because such movements were usually attempted by cavalry, ski troops and infantry mounted on sleighs who were unable to take their heavy weapons with them. The striking power that the Russian forces were able to bring forward was not sufficient to destroy the defender.

Russian Tactics

The Russians usually attacked along existing roads or on paths beaten down by their tanks. Frequently, the infantry followed close behind their tanks, using the trail made by the tank tracks. In other instances infantry worked its way forward in snow tunnels toward German positions, despite the heavy losses which resulted from such tactics. In mass attacks the Russians usually debouched from woods and burrowed their way through the deep snow as quickly as possible. Mowed down by machine guns, the first wave would be followed by a second attack which moved forward a short distance over the bodies of the dead before coming to a standstill. This was repeated by as many as ten waves, until the Russians bogged down from heavy losses and exhaustion or until the German defenses were penetrated.

Russian infiltration tactics were most effective in winter, because the German defense system, based on strong points, practically invited such tactics. The Germans were forced to adopt the strong point system of defense because they lacked sufficient forces to occupy continuous lines backed up by reserves. The Russians always sought to split and annihilate defending forces, and to this end cavalry, ski units. airborne troops, and, above all, partisans were used in great numbers.

I. Ski Troops

On the night of 20-21 March 1942, six hundred Russian ski troops enveloped the command post of the 269th Division in a village twelve miles northeast of Lyuban. The flanking movement was made under cover of darkness over a bog which had a weak bearing surface and was therefore but lightly guarded by the Germans. As these troops assaulted the rear of the village, heavy attacks with armored support were launched against the entire division front. After a bitter fight, division service troops managed to drive off the ski troops.

Another instance of Russian use of strong ski forces occurred at the end of March 1942, after 6th Panzer Division had captured several villages southwest of Rzhev in a limited-objective attack. The area was immediately organized for defense; roads were cleared in the three-foot-deep snow, and paths cleared to the numerous bunkers taken in the action.

Under cover of darkness, a ski brigade of the Russian Thirty-ninth Guards Army, under command of a general officer, assembled in a wooded area opposite a strong point held by the

114th Panzer Grenadier Regiment plus an artillery battalion and some flak. At daybreak, the ski brigade attacked the German position, with the main effort against the German rear. The defenders recognized the Russian intentions and withheld fire until the attackers came within two to three hundred yards. The Germans then opened fire with 500 rifles, 36 machine guns, and 16 artillery pieces. The effect was devastating. Such of the enemy as survived buried themselves in the snow in the hope of returning to the woods at night. Most of the weapons and all of the ski equipment of the force engaged in the main attack were captured. The greatest prize, however, was a map found on the dead commander which gave the disposition of the entire Thirty-ninth Guards Army.

The Russians failed in their mission because they could not achieve surprise. In cold weather sound travels a great distance, and their approach over the snow could clearly be heard. Furthermore, the attack carried across open terrain and all the roads and paths around the German positions were well guarded.

Russian ski units were more successful when used in combination with other arms. When Third Panzer Army was withdrawing west of Moscow in December 1941, a Russian force composed of ski troops, cavalry, and sleigh-mounted infantry succeeded in cutting off the 6th Panzer Division which was the rear guard of LVI Panzer Corps.

II. Unusual Russian Tactics

In October 1941 a Russian force crossed the ice-covered Gulf of Finland from Leningrad and made a surprise attack on the 212th Infantry Division. The attack, made under cover of darkness in a driving snowstorm, was thrown back to the shore after a stiff fight. The Russians had marched eastward across the ice from Leningrad to Kronshtadt and then southward to hit the German flank and rear.

Similarly, at the end of January 1945 the Russians tried to unhinge the left flank of Third Panzer Army, which was on the

Deime River, by envelopment across the ice of the Kurisches Haff. Three times the enemy penetrated the army front as far as the town of Labiau, and each time was thrown back after hard fighting.

In the winter of 1941-42 the Russians supplied Leningrad day after day with food and ammunition by using an ice road over Lake Ladoga. The ice road, eighteen miles long, was nine to twelve miles from the southern shore. At night the same road was used to move regiments and even divisions from Leningrad to the Eighth and Fifty-fourth Russian Armies. The Germans fired 150-mm. artillery against the ice road, but could not stop the Russians. They continued moving troops and supplies despite all losses.

Clothing, Equipment, Rations
I. Clothing

In the winter of 1941-42, the most severe in Russia in a hundred years, the Germans, if they had any winter clothing at all, carried only the regular issue overcoat, sweater, belly-band, and hood designed for winter wear in Germany. The bulk of the winter garments donated by the German people did not reach the front until the end of January 1942, after cold had done its damage. Frostbite casualties were numerous. For instance, a panzer division near Volokolamsk in January 1942 had up to 800 frostbite casualties a day.

During the inactivity of the autumn 1941 muddy period, fur pieces and felt boots were manufactured locally, purchased from civilians, or removed from dead Russian soldiers; but these sources supplied only a small number of troops. All available underwear was issued so that several sets could be worn at one time, and each man managed to obtain a piece of cloth for use as a belly-band or head protector. Some Germans acquired Russian-type fur caps, which proved dangerous, since, despite the addition of distinguishing insignia, the wearers were often mistaken for enemy and fired upon by friendly troops.

After the first winter of the war, clothing supplies improved, and although items lacked uniformity of appearance they served their purpose. Garments were worn in various combinations, such as: heavy quilted trousers, fur vest, regular jacket, and regular overcoat; quilted trousers, sweater, quilted jacket, and regular overcoat; heavy quilted trousers, sweater, regular jacket, and fur coat; or regular trousers, knee protectors, regular jacket, and fur coat. With these combinations each man wore warm underwear, gloves, scarf, and felt or felt-and-leather boots.

The Germans found the quilted suit with hood, worn over the regular uniform, plus a fur cap, felt boots with leather reinforcement or leather soles, and fur gloves best for cold weather. This was the type of winter uniform worn by the Russians. Long sheepskin coats should be worn by drivers and guards. Without winter clothing troops cannot remain out of doors in temperatures under -10° F.

White camouflage clothing should have some identifying feature. Whiteclad German ski formations moving at extended order through wooded areas, or advancing during snowstorms, were sometimes infiltrated by similarly dressed Russian troops.

II. Equipment
Weapons
Maintenance of weapons is difficult in winter. German rifles and machine guns developed malfunctions because the grease and oil used were not cold-resistant. Strikers and striker springs broke like glass; fluid in artillery recoil mechanisms solidified, crippling the piece. Light weapons had to be warmed in huts, and fires were lighted under the barrels of guns to get them back into action. Before suitable lubricants were available, troops found an emergency solution in the removal of every trace of grease and oil from their weapons. In the south of Russia, the abundantly available sunflower oil was used as a lubricant. It is acid-free and cold-resistant.

Vehicles

The need for spare motor vehicle and tank parts increases at low temperatures. The number of broken . springs, for instance, reached unusually high proportions. The Germans cannibalized broken-down and abandoned vehicles to get spare parts. The policy of furnishing as many complete tanks and motor vehicles as possible to the front was detrimental to spare parts production. It was by no means unusual that some armored regiments sent their technical personnel on unauthorized trips to factories in Germany to obtain spare parts through personal contact.

Winter temperatures in Russia render self-starters useless. The Germans resorted to prewarming engines by building fires under them. In this way a few vehicles were started for towing. During alerts motors were frequently kept running for hours.

III. Rations

During winter, particular attention must be given to proper packaging and storage of foods sensitive to cold. At extreme low temperatures the Germans found that even the relatively short haul from field kitchens to men on the line sufficed to turn food into lumps of ice. Foods sensitive to heat kept almost indefinitely in cold weather.

Transportation and Troop Movements

I. Roads

During winter, road conditions are usually favorable except during bad weather. Roads kept free of snow are easily passable, often better than in summer. With the onset of heavy snowfalls, however, difficulties arose on all traffic routes, which were counteracted by the road services of the various German armies. The assignment of one battalion per thirty miles of road proved satisfactory for snow clearance. Civilian labor was hired for shoveling and for driving horse-drawn plows.

At certain points along roads the Germans established relay stations to provide warm quarters and food for drivers and small units that were held up by snowstorms. Other stations, manned by engineer personnel, were in telephone communication with corps and army, to which road conditions were reported by 0800 each day. Army distributed daily bulletins with maps showing road conditions.

If at all possible, each emergency station had one motorized snowplow. Two or three motorized snowplows were held in reserve by army to clear the way for important troop movements. It was the German experience that during severe snowstorms at least six power plows were necessary to keep a road open for an infantry division. Strong winds caused snowdrifts which blocked all traffic. Shoveling during storms was futile, for the roads quickly became covered again. To avoid drifts the Germans routed winter roads through woods, where drifts rarely occur, or along the crest of high ground, where the snow is usually less deep.

Snow Fences

Whenever roads across open terrain must be used, snow fences should be erected before the beginning of winter. The location of snow fences is important. They must be set up on both sides of the road, fifty to seventy feet from the shoulders. After a snowstorm the fences must be placed on top of the snow wall that has formed behind them.

In most instances the prewar snow fences had disappeared, and fences four to five feet high had to be improvised out of latticework, wickerwork, or branches of coniferous trees. If materials for construction of snow fences were not available, the Germans used snow blocks.

Marking of Roads

If snow roads follow a different course from those indicated on maps, they should be marked on the ground so they can be followed after a heavy snowfall or when covered by drifted snow. The Germans marked roads with tall poles topped with straw or branches. Stakes with black or red tops or colored markers were also used.

Ice-covered Roads

Serious traffic jams are often caused by icy roads. It is important to have towing service ready to render assistance in icy sections. In hilly terrain the Germans set up sand dumps, and all vehicles were ordered to carry sand. Vehicles with trailers were barred from icy roads, since they often became stuck even if roads were sanded.

II. Railroads

Heavy snowfalls and drifting snow interrupt railway traffic, and the Germans used local civilian labor and snowplows to keep tracks clear. Cold reduced the efficiency of German locomotives which had been built for the milder temperatures of Central Europe. During the first winter of the war 70 percent of the German locomotives broke down. Only after a period of trial and error and protracted technical research which led to the introduction of a new type of locomotive, did the Germans overcome their difficulties. Railroad construction and maintenance requiring excavation slowed down or stopped completely in cold weather. Cold crippled operations, caused traffic congestion, and slowed supply movement.

In the winter of 1941-42, sometimes only one third, and frequently less, of the daily quota of twenty-eight trains got through to Army Group Center. The German Second Army and Second Panzer Army together required eighteen supply trains a day and received only two. In November 1941 these armies were unable to take Tula because their supply system had broken down. Even the most critical supplies did not reach the front in time.

III. Draft Horses

Most of the German horses became accustomed to the Russian winter, although they needed at least emergency shelter. In the open, horses freeze to death at temperatures under -4° F. Russian horses, with their thick shaggy winter coat can withstand temperatures as low as -58° F. if they are sheltered against the

Soldier with machine-pistol and white winter coat, with a cart horse in Russia, 1941.

wind. Some German horses, notably the heavy cold-blooded breeds, were unable to withstand the Russian winter, particularly those moved suddenly from the mild climate of France.

The Germans expected their draft horses to pull excessive loads in winter, and the animals became prematurely spent particularly when they were given insufficient care, forage, and water. Lighter breeds were better able to stand the cold, but were not strong enough to move the heavy German equipment; they became exhausted, and collapsed and died in the snow.

During the first winter of the war German horses frequently lacked winter shoeing, a factor which lessened their draft power on icy roads and caused them to fall. Sometimes ice was so bad that horses which had not been wintershod could not be led from the railroad station to the stables.

A great many horses perished for lack of forage. In quiet sectors horses were worked as little as possible when feed was short. Work teams which were given extra feed were used for routine duties.

There were no horse diseases directly traceable to or

aggravated by the Russian winter. Most of the 1,500,000 horses which the Germans lost in Russia were victims of battle wounds, overexertion, forage shortages, and cold.

Health and Morale
I. Evacuation of Casualties
In some respects conditions for evacuation of casualties during winter were more favorable than during other seasons. Even after a heavy snow, road traffic was soon restored. In some sectors native sleighs were used for evacuation, and special sleighs with enclosed wooden superstructures were built and did good service. Battlefield evacuation was done with small one-man sleds which are easily pulled by one or two soldiers.

A plentiful supply of blankets is essential, and the Germans also used paper coverings to protect limbs of casualties in transit. Frost injuries rarely occurred during evacuation, and only during the first year of the war, when hospital trains were immobilized for hours by cold, did wounded freeze to death. Except for the length of time involved, evacuation generally caused little discomfort to casualties.

II. Effect of Cold on Morale
The reverses suffered at Moscow lowered the morale of both officers and men who felt that lack of preparation for winter warfare was the cause of their defeat. Although it was too late to correct the basic mistakes, officers succeeded in convincing troops that the retreat would soon end, and that defeat would not become disaster.

Many men who had become separated from their units marched westward singly or in small groups and, when apprehended, freely admitted that their destination was Germany because 'the war is over.' These men were turned over to the nearest combat unit for rehabilitation. More serious were the cases of deserters who concealed themselves on farms and managed to obtain civilian clothes. The number of deserters to the enemy was few.

Since gasoline was precious, thefts of fuel were common. Troops helped themselves wherever they found unguarded stocks, and even drained tanks of unattended vehicles. Spare parts were scarce and were stolen whenever it was opportune to do so.

Air Operations
I. Aircraft

In general, German aircraft stood up well even under the worst winter conditions. However, oil became quite viscous, and placed an excessive strain on various parts, especially hydraulic equipment, and a special type of winter hydraulic fluid had to be used. Lubricating oil was heated before starting engines, and electric storage batteries were also prewarmed because cold reduced their efficiency.

Aircraft tires did not show adverse effects at temperatures down to -30° F, but at lower temperatures tires started to become porous. Other rubber parts, such as self-sealing tanks and rubber packings of shock absorbers, deteriorated when exposed to prolonged, intense cold. Tarpaulins provided good weather cover for wings and tail units of aircraft parked in the open, and served as camouflage.

The Germans kept some planes in heated 'alarm boxes' during periods of low temperatures to assure an immediate take-off during an alarm. Skis were installed on light liaison planes for landings away from airfields. Combat aircraft took off on wheels from packed-down runways.

II. Airfields

For winter operations, air installations must have adequate, heated working space, heating equipment, snow-removal, and snow-packing equipment, and good quarters. The Germans found that aircraft maintenance in winter took several times as long as in summer unless heated working space was available.

Concrete runways and strips quickly become covered with snow, and careful maintenance through packing and removal of excess snow is necessary. Since snow in many areas of Russia remains dry and powdery throughout the winter, excessive snowdrifts pile up whenever there is a strong wind. All obstacles must be cleared from runways, for even small bushes and gasoline drums may be the cause of drifts several feet high.

In view of possible changes in plans involving the redistribution of units and the movement of reinforcements, the Germans tried to keep even unused airfields ready for winter operation. To get fields into operation once winter had set in required a considerable expenditure of time and labor and sometimes necessitated the construction of roads if no railroad connection was available for movement of materiel.

III. Flight

The very short days of winter made night flying necessary for extended missions. German crews not qualified for night flying were therefore limited to missions of short duration.

Particular difficulties were encountered in orientation from the air because of the similarity of snow-covered ground to snow cover on frozen lakes and rivers. During winter -as well as during spring floods and mud -the Russian landscape bears little resemblance to what is shown on maps. New aerial photographic maps and sketches for each season are indispensable for navigation and for effective co-operation with ground forces.

During early winter, ceilings and visibility below the clouds are usually favorable enough to permit flights along coastal areas. Poor visibility and clouds resembling high altitude fog frequently appear within the cold continental air masses and western warm air masses over the Volkhov River and Lake Peipus. The danger of ice formation during all seasons is greater in European Russia than in Central Europe. Frequently when Germany and western Russia have good flying weather the intermediate area of eastern Poland has low overcasts, poor visibility, precipitation, and conditions which lead to formation of ice.

In the German experience the number of accidents caused by climatic conditions in Russia was neither greater nor less than in Central Europe. Emergency missions necessitated by the ground situation, such as low-level attacks to support armor, or supply flights—especially to Stalingrad—naturally brought about increased losses attributable to weather conditions. Virtually every emergency landing in winter resulted in total loss of the aircraft.

IV. Emergency Equipment

Based on the experiences gained in the first winter of the war, normal emergency equipment was supplemented by short skis with which flight crews could cover considerable distances if forced down. Snowshoes proved unsatisfactory and consequently ski boots were issued instead of air force fur-lined boots. Equipment for emergency landings in all seasons included abundant quantities of salt and pictures of saints which were used as barter items with the local population.

V. Rations and Clothing

The campaign in Russia taught the Germans nothing basically new in the matter of rations for flight personnel. Standard preparations for long-range and high-altitude flight assured that personnel were properly fed for extreme climatic conditions.

Normal-issue cold-weather clothing was adequate for flight and maintenance personnel.

NORTH OF THE ARCTIC CIRCLE

General

The Arctic zone of European Russia extends from the arctic coast east of Kirkenes southward to the Bay of Kandalaksha, a distance of about 190 air miles. This area contains the southward routes of land communication from Murmansk and commands the shipping lanes to the White Sea ports. Climatic conditions in this land of midnight sun and polar night pose serious problems not only in the conduct of military operations, but also for mere survival.

North of the Arctic Circle the conduct of operations is circumscribed by time and space elements unknown in temperate-regions. The midnight sun of summer, the twenty-four-hour night of winter, and the muddy transition periods of spring and autumn nullify conventional concepts of freedom of maneuver.

In the arctic a military decision communicated by an order is irrevocable. Whatever forces have been committed, whatever course of action has been initiated, an interminable time elapses between original impulse and final effect. Once started, the chain reaction must run its course. To stop, to reverse, to change direction is to run the risk of losing the initiative. First decisions must be correct. Command procedure must be adapted to the unorthodoxies of warfare in the north. Leaders at all levels, down to the squad, must make decisions far transcending the scope of their usual responsibilities.

North of the Arctic Circle the enormous land mass of European Russia, with its wide seasonal range in temperature, borders on the Barents Sea region which is moderated by the warm current of the Atlantic Drift. While the oceanic influence is strongest in the fjords on the arctic coast, the continental climate of interior Russia dominates the inland sea. A comparison of mean temperatures in northern Karelia with those in corresponding latitudes in Siberia strikingly illustrates the influence of the Atlantic Drift. In winter, for example, this warm current raises the level of mean temperatures by at least 35° F., and, through the warming influence of the sea quickly decreases toward the interior, the January mean in the inland area of the Kola Peninsula is still 18° F. higher than in corresponding latitudes of Siberia.

The mean winter temperature on the Murman coast, 13° F., is the same as the January mean at Minneapolis, Minnesota. The mean temperature during July—the hottest month—is 53° F., equal to the average May temperature on the North Sea coast of Central Europe. The comparison, however, applies only to mean values; actual day-to-day variations in temperature are substantially greater and much more abrupt than in Central Europe. In winter a transition from thaw to severe frost may be a matter of a few hours, and the mercury may rise again just as suddenly. Winter readings on the arctic coast range from 43° to -31° F. Summer maximums on the coast vary between 75° and 85° F., with temperatures in the interior rising as high as 95° F. Night frosts are nevertheless fairly common during the subpolar summer. Only the coastal region has one whole month of temperatures above freezing—July.

Generally speaking, there are but two seasons north of the Arctic Circle: the long, cold, and dark winter; and the short summer with no night. The ideal time for large-scale ground operations is late winter, the two-month period beginning around March. At that time the days grow longer, lakes and swamps are still frozen, and ice roads can be used to move men and materiel. Early winter, right after the formation of ice, is also favorable, but an operation in early winter runs the risk of continuing into the adverse conditions of the polar night. Summer is the season least suited to ground operations. Large areas of the terrain are impassable and the land routes of the arctic are in the worst possible condition at this time.

Housing is virtually nonexistent in the high latitudes of European Russia. Finnish-type log huts are best for permanent quarters up to latitude 69° N-, and farther north timbered dugouts are best. The Germans found collapsible wooden barracks useful throughout the north. Snow is usually too loose and powdery for igloos, and ordinary shelter tents are inadequate. The Finnish plywood tent and the Swedish cloth tent with stoves are excellent, and in emergencies snow-covered windbreaks having pine-bough roofs and heated by low reflecting fires offer good protection.

Section I. Infantry

Small unit actions, away from established front lines, are feasible in the desolate arctic. The limited visibility of the polar night favors operations at company, battalion, or, in exceptional cases, regimental strength. Operations are usually of limited duration, because every bit of equipment must be carried along. Only troops in excellent physical condition can be used. Fighting and inarching through wasteland, forest tangle, and brush demands endurance, esprit de corps and the ability to exploit every terrain feature to the utmost.

The Germans learned that only mountain and ski troops should be used' in the arctic, and that such troops are most effective when organized in ski units or mobile task forces. The mobile task force should include both combat and supply elements, and a large percentage of its personnel should be equipped with skis to prevent the force from becoming roadbound. Its heavy weapons should be suitable for break down into one-man loads for the same reason. Ski units should be capable of at least three days of combat in any kind of terrain without resupply.

Visibility in the close terrain of the arctic is so poor that the Germans were forced to organize infantry observation battalions to direct tire of infantry howitzers and mortars. Captive balloons were also used for observation. The XXXVI Mountain Corps, on the Kandalaksha front, had a permanently attached balloon section.

Finnish Tactics

Finnish units in the arctic operated with what they called Sissi and Motti tactics which are planned to permit small, battle-seasoned units to fight on even terms against numerically superior forces.

Sissi combat denotes small unit actions which have the objective of hitting the enemy at one point. Each participant is briefed on the objective, and the method of execution is left up to the group.

Motti tactics are, on a small scale, analogous to the envelopment tactics of German doctrine. Motti uses small forces for enveloping—almost sneaking around—the enemy, and attacking and annihilating him once the ring has been closed.

Both methods take advantage of concealment, defilade, and flank protection offered by lakes and watercourses, and depend upon the self reliance, initiative, and fighting spirit of officers and men.

Commando-type Actions

Commando-type missions in the arctic require highly trained special purpose units. Finnish troops who raided the Russian-held Murmansk railway were specially trained and equipped.

The Russians dropped parachutists, including female radio operators, behind the German lines. The presence of these Russian teams usually became known only through interception of radio messages.

Section II. Artillery

Artillery for the virtually roadless arctic must be light and mobile. Long-range artillery is useless in close terrain. The Germans entered the arctic campaign of World War II with divisional artillery that required Jen horses for displacement and GHQ artillery that included 175-mm. and 280-mm. pieces. These were soon supplemented with light and medium mortars because the big guns had no targets at which to fire. The Germans used antitank guns to knock out enemy bunkers above ground, while the Russians used antiaircraft artillery against ground targets.

In winter, artillery can be displaced over ice. Many Russian attempts to cross ice under cover of darkness were foiled by the German method of stationing sound-ranging teams, equipped with seismological instruments, at the edge of frozen lakes to detect enemy movement.

Generally, German artillery techniques in the arctic were no different than those used in winter in the lower latitudes of European Russia.

III. Armored Forces

Tanks and self-propelled artillery are of limited value in the arctic region of European Russia. Huge granite boulders cover the landscape, making cross-country operations impossible. Armor can be moved only on the few available roads. No German tank or self-propelled gun ever saw action north of the Arctic Circle in World War II.

The climatic conditions of the arctic can be and were mastered by the Germans who were able to learn many lessons from the Finns, but nevertheless had to go through bitter experiences of their own. The observations on polar warfare presented in this study were drawn from both sources. A number of other lessons, such as the reorganization of units for arctic warfare, special training, the flow of replacements, and Russian and Finnish combat methods are treated in CMH Pub 104-1, Military Improvisations During the Russian Campaign; CMH Pub 104-12, Russian Combat Methods in World War II; and CMH Pub 104-24, Warfare in the Far North.

Clothing, Equipment, Rations
I. Clothing

Winter uniforms must be designed to give protection against the extreme cold of the arctic region. The Germans found several layers of clothing better than merely thick, heavy apparel. Trousers should fit loosely enough to permit wearing of at least two pairs of drawers; trouser legs should be cut full around the calf and fit tightly about the ankle. Blouses must be large enough to be worn over extra underwear and a fur vest. Windproof, snowproof parkas are essential for ski troops. Chemical warming pads inserted under clothing add to physical comfort. Fur outer clothing is required for sentries, drivers, and others engaged in limited physical activity. Fur clothing is not suitable for ski troops because it induces perspiration; quilted uniforms are best for ski wear. A wool toque plus a felt or fur cap with ear flaps is best for winter. White camouflage coats or coveralls are essential for combat troops, and the Germans also found white face masks useful. Camouflage covers are needed for headgear. For summer wear in the arctic, the regular uniform plus a mosquito veil and sunglasses proved adequate.

The jagged rocks, swamps, and snow of the arctic require sturdy, waterproof boots, which should be adaptable for skiing. Only boots of top-grade, double-stitched leather give adequate protection against frostbite and trenchfoot. Russians taken prisoner complained that l their U. S. army boots were not water-repellent, were in adequately stitched, and were generally unsuited to arctic wear. Ski boots must be large enough to permit extra socks and felt inner soles to be worn. The best ski boot is double-stitched with a long tongue that is securely stitched to the upper, and full leather sole under a ribbed composition sole. Soles should extend beyond the sides of the toe caps and be covered with brass inserts. Canvas leggings provide good protection in loose, deep snow.

Fur-lined boots large enough to accommodate heat packets are needed for sentries, and drivers should have felt boots. Lapp shoes, soft shoes made of reindeer hide, are needed by ski troops for tent wear. A limited quantity of rubber boots, enough for about 15 percent of combat personnel, is required for thaw and muddy periods and for occasional summer wear.

II. Equipment
Individual Equipment
In the arctic the primary consideration is not how much the individual can carry, but how much he can possibly leave behind without impairing his chances for survival. The German soldier undoubtedly presented a more military appearance than the Finn or Russian, but many of the German items turned out to be mere ballast. About all the Finnish soldier carried was a rifle or

submachine gun and a dagger on his belt. He carried no gas mask, no steel helmet, no bayonet. For construction of shelter and clearance of trails combat troops need saws or hatchets that can be carried on the rucksack or pack. The Finnish oil-filled wrist compass is best for extreme temperatures, but even this type compass is subject to serious deviations due to natural mineral deposits and the effects of the aurora borealis.

Pack Equipment

The rucksack is the best pack for the arctic. It offers less interference in passing through narrow clefts or underbrush, and is more comfortable for skiing. The Germans found that forty pounds is the maximum which should be carried on lengthy missions; heavier loads impair speed and mobility.

Ski Equipment

Most ski movement in the arctic is over flat terrain, and skis should therefore be light and narrow, about two and one-half inches wide, without reinforced edges. Tips should be slightly turned and holes provided for pull ropes. Snow should be used for camouflage, since paint dries skis and leads to damage, A simple cross-country binding is best for arctic use.

The Germans found steel ski poles with tightly woven webbing adequate, although steel deflects compasses. Ski climbers are necessary when pulling sleds or similar loads. An important item for ski troops is a small tool kit, about one per squad, for emergency repairs.

Snowshoes

Snowshoes are needed for personnel carrying heavy loads. The Germans found that wooden-frame snowshoes with leather webbing rendered excellent service, while snowshoes with willow webbing proved unsatisfactory.

Small Arms

In the wilderness of the north, where the fire fight is usually carried on at close range, a high cyclic rate of fire in small arms is more important than accuracy. The submachine gun is ideal for arctic combat. The early type of German submachine gun frequently jammed at low temperatures and, until an improved design was brought out, German troops preferred to use the Russian model. In extreme cold air-cooled weapons are superior to water-cooled. Ammunition was usually a critical item for Germans in the arctic, and strict fire discipline was maintained. A plentiful supply of ammunition for a Jaw weapons is better than many weapons with little ammunition. German experiences with small arms in the arctic differed little from those in Russia generally.

Hand Grenades

The stick hand grenade was found to be unsafe in the arctic; it catches on trees and rocks, and the Germans replaced it with egg-type grenades. Deep snow renders grenade bursts harmless.

Mortars

Ski troops effectively employed 81-mm. mortars. Medium mortar shells are effective, even in deep snow.

Radio Equipment

Arctic warfare consists mostly of small unit actions, and therefore great reliance must be placed on radio communications. German equipment was too bulky and too limited in range for arctic use, and the small, powerful American-made equipment used by the Finns was much better. The component parts of signal equipment must be adaptable to pack-animal transport.

Low temperatures damage storage batteries, and the Germans cradled them between heating pads to preserve their power. Troops starting on extended missions should take freshly charged batteries.

Radio communications in the arctic are disturbed by the aurora borealis and by magnetic fields.

Vehicles

Motor vehicles must have good ground clearance to permit passage over rocks and boulders which protrude from such roads as are found in the arctic. Roads are too narrow to allow passing, and long drives in low gear strain engines and transmission. Starting vehicles required the same precautions as those used by the Germans in European Russia below the Arctic Circle. Fascine mats are useful in mud and snow, and adequate stocks of snow chains and sled runners are important.

German horse-drawn wagons are suited only for movement over roads, and found little use in the arctic. The two-wheeled Finnish cart drawn by one native horse is well adapted to arctic conditions. Terrain impassable for wheeled vehicles can be traversed by the purilla, a sledge fashioned from a forked bough or two slender tree trunks. The purilla can easily be pulled over rocks and mud and can tarry twice the payload of a pack animal.

The Finnish peasant horse sleigh is practical for arctic use, as are the Finnish akja and loijakka. The akja is a small boat-shaped sled which weighs about thirty pounds, readily glides over obstacles, and always maintains a steady balance. The loijakka is a larger akja, and is suitable for moving bulky cargo. Both are usually drawn by reindeer, though they can be pulled by ski personnel. Two men can pull 100 pounds in flat country, and three men can pull the same load in mountainous terrain.

Motorized combat sleighs armed with a heavy machine gun and carrying three to five men were extensively used by the Russians. The Germans made a few experiments with this type of equipment. The German models were successful only on frozen lakes with a thin snow cover.

III. Rations

The rigors of the arctic require foods which provide extra energy. The Germans issued extra fats and bread, while the Finns relied on extra rations of sugar. German winter food supplies consisted of frozen beef, pork, and vegetables; dehydrated potatoes and legumes; cheese and canned foods. Since the Baltic Sea was usually blocked all winter, food was stocked in advance for an entire year.

Transportation and Troop Movements
I. Roads

There are few roads in the arctic wilderness. On the Kandalaksha front in World War II a sector extending 250 miles in a north-south direction contained only one east-west road which, by European or even Russian standards, was not a road at all.

Scouts probing into enemy territory had to mark out a route of advance for infantry. Later, construction troops transformed the track into a wagon trail. At first, the wagon trail would be the only supply route, and thousands of hours of work were needed to widen the trail to accommodate horse-drawn vehicles and trucks. The Finns had some American road-building machinery which was most helpful.

The Germans found that a corps needed two to four battalions of engineer troops to maintain roads once they were built. Jagged rocks constantly worked to the surface, and in muddy terrain corduroy or chespaling had to be used.

During summer the numerous lakes, swamps, and rivers of the arctic make large-scale operations entirely dependent upon man-made routes of communication. Progress is inevitably slow. Sometimes the enemy is able to control available roads so effectively that only wide envelopment, sometimes upward of ten miles laterally, can reduce his positions and open the way for the advance of friendly forces. For instance, in the summer of 1941, when the Germans were inexperienced in arctic warfare, the Russians blocked the sole route through the wilderness to Kandalaksha with a line of bunkers reinforced by artillery, while the road itself was patrolled by tanks. Any German maneuver short of wide envelopment would have meant a costly hammering at the Russian positions. Wide envelopment, however, required construction of paths for the main attack and trails for the secondary close-in envelopments. The Germans found that every one of four twelve-mile advances in the operation required four weeks of preparation for seven days of combat.

Terrain difficulties are less pronounced in winter, when frozen lakes, swamps, and rivers become good routes of communication.

Snow and Ice Roads

An ice cover of three feet or more on a lake supports the heaviest loads, and the Germans made ice roads by simply clearing snow with a conventional or rotary snow plow.

Snow roads were built over swamps by removing snow and then pouring water over the cleared surface until a frozen surface was built up. The Russians used forty-four regiments in the construction of snow roads on the Kandalaksha front in 1944. Each man was made responsible for about five square yards a day, and in this manner two 65-miles stretches were completed virtually overnight.

Snow clearance was carried out and snow fences were built in the same way as in other parts of Russia.

II. Railroads

Locomotives for arctic use must be designed to burn wood, the only fuel available in high latitudes. Locomotives equipped with snow plows were used to keep railroads open, and in one instance the Germans converted a Russian tank into a motor-driven armored railway car that was equipped for double duty as a snow plow. Russian and Finnish railroads are broad gauge.

Railroads over ice

In the winter of 1941-42 the Baltic froze over, completely cutting off German forces in Finland from sea communication with their homeland. Even the most powerful Swedish ice breakers were unable to get through. A plan for a railroad over the ice from Reval to Helsinki, similar to the Russian undertaking on Lake Ladoga, was abandoned because the ice of the Baltic was constantly in motion. The Finns attempted unsuccessfully to move motorized columns across the narrowest part of the Gulf of Bothnia in the winter of 1939-40.

SdKfz 10/5 variant, with 2 cm Flak 38 gun, Russia, November 1943

III. Ski and Dismounted Movement

Ski marches are the most practical form of movement during winter. In difficult terrain with a moderately deep snow cover, the Germans found that small units should not exceed two to two and one-half miles per hour, and larger units about one and one-half miles per hour. Foot troops should move about one-half mile per hour, or about one-third mile per hour when carrying loads or evacuating casualties. Unreasonable speed on skis or on foot stimulates perspiration and induces chills and frostbite.

IV. Draft and Pack Animals

Heavy, cold-blooded horses lack the stamina required for service in the arctic. Finnish, Esthonian, and the small Norwegian horses proved best for pack and draft duty. Mere windbreaks suffice for their shelter, and they readily accept thawed-out hay. Sickness among horses was rare.

The reindeer is a better work animal than the horse in the arctic. It is efficient in deep snow, gets along with very little forage, and needs little shelter. Despite the reindeer's normal self-sufficiency, pasturage must be selected in advance of the winter season, and moss and similar forage gathered to avoid starvation in case of unusually deep snow.

Horse-sleighs carry packets of tobacco near Orel, Russia, December 1941

Only reindeer broken to harness are suitable for military purposes. Trained reindeer are capable of pulling 150 to 250 pounds up to thirty-five miles a day, with one day's rest alternating with two days' work. As a pack animal, the reindeer can carry forty to sixty pounds. In deep snow it is advisable to have skiers break trail for reindeer.

By late spring, the reindeer reverts to its wild state of roaming the forest, and does not seek contact with man until the autumn. The reindeer cannot endure a strange scent, and can be handled only by its owner. It even refuses to drink except from its individual water hole.

Health and Morale
I. Health
Lack of sunshine during the long polar night causes deficiency symptoms, and the Germans rigidly supervised daily administration of vitamins, particularly vitamin C and cod liver oil.

German troops in the arctic suffered kidney diseases, perhaps as a result of colds, although Finnish medical authorities spoke of the presence of a communicable kidney ailment. Leptospirosis, a communicable sickness of about twelve-days' duration, and having malaria-like symptoms, was widespread. This disease was attributed to contact with the excrement of lemmings, mole-like brown and white rodents.

The sauna, or steam bath, was widely used by the Germans. It toughens the body and builds up resistance to the arctic climate. Its regular use not only helps prevent colds and rheumatic ailments, but also constitutes a vital morale booster in cases of so-called Lapp-happiness, the melancholia which may be induced by the monotony of midnight sun and polar night.

German troops in the arctic were adequately clothed, and frostbite casualties were rare. Nonbattle casualties in the arctic during the entire war amounted to only about 2 percent of total troop strength, a figure which compared favorably with that of the best health years of peacetime.

Medical Care

The Germans found that during the polar night prompt treatment and evacuation of casualties, no matter how lightly injured, was essential to speedy recovery. Early medical aid could be rendered only if skilled medical personnel were immediately available, and procedures were devised for rendering first aid on combat patrols, at strong points, and on the firing line. The difficulties were many. Casualties were often far from established positions, roads were few, and footpaths were narrow and rocky. Young, able-bodied medical officers were attached to combat troops, and only doctors able to ski were picked for such duty. Some enlisted medical personnel were given advanced training in first aid and assigned to combat troops when no medical officers were available.

Evacuation

Finding and evacuating casualties in deep snow or close terrain is difficult, and the Germans sometimes used dogs to track down wounded or injured personnel. Evacuation was accomplished on stretcher frames slung between two horses hitched in tandem, by purilla, or by single-wheel mountain litter. Reindeer were also used to pull the akja in evacuation operations.

Emergency sleds for evacuation can be fashioned from skis, using ski adapters or ski poles. Dog teams were used for evacuation over flat or gently rolling terrain. Evacuation by litter bearers was slow, and required large numbers of personnel. Casualties located in extremely inaccessible parts of the wilderness were frequently evacuated by aircraft. In winter frozen lakes provided landing areas, and in summer lakes were used for hydroplane landings.

II. Morale

The psychological strain of the twenty-four-hour summer day and the seemingly endless polar night had an adverse effect on troop morale. The Germans found that combat personnel past their mid-twenties were more affected by arctic conditions than younger troops.

Whenever possible the Germans, to raise morale, encouraged hunting, fishing, regular use of the sauna bath, and provided the opportunity for soldiers to cook a meal of their own choice.

The use of distinctive insignia for arctic troops bolsters morale considerably.

Air Operations

I. General

If proper preparations are made, air operations can be conducted the year round in the arctic. In summer, each lake is a sheltered water landing and, in winter when frozen over, an excellent landing field for aircraft of moderate size. With air superiority and suitable landing areas, air transport is an important factor in supplying advanced ground units and in relieving other supply facilities. Small units can be supplied by airdrop.

It is difficult to camouflage air installations in the far north. There are either huge wooded areas into which the profile of an airfield cuts sharply or the terrain is bare and rocky, and thus susceptible to enemy observation. The German remedy in the latter instance was to hollow bunkers and hangars out of the rocks.

Latticed wooden runways were used with success by the Germans during the spring and autumn muddy periods. When this was done aircraft were, of necessity, parked near the landing strips; construction of latticed taxi strips would have involved tremendous extra effort.

II. Flight

Snow covers all irregularities in the terrain during winter, ice makes coastal boundaries indistinct, and orientation during flight is generally difficult. Flat vapor and fog layers seen from the air are difficult to distinguish from snow.

Warm fronts from over the Atlantic are frequent in January. These fronts produce heavy cloud formations over land and sea, fog that extends to high altitudes, and scattered rain or snow. Icing and poor visibility result.

Over the Arctic Ocean ice will begin to form at 6,500 feet,, even in summer. During spring and autumn ice forms at very low altitudes in cloud formations, and in winter this danger increases. In winter even comparatively thin cloud layers produce snow.

In extremely cold weather, pools of very cold, dense air form over the interior of fjords. If a strong wind blows across a fjord at a certain angle, some of this cold air will be sucked out, and replaced by warmer air from above. This process can cause a violent storm in a matter of minutes, with winds of high velocity accompanied by a sudden rise in temperature.

Modern air forces may revolutionize arctic warfare. In summer every lake provides a convenient water landing; in winter an extensive airfield. Anticipatory measures to use the arctic for air operations can be taken at any time. Such preparations can counteract to some extent the difficulties presented by lack of overland routes and the inhospitality of the polar region. Even with extensive use of aircraft, the lessons presented in this study will remain valid.

Conclusions

Combat in European Russia was greatly influenced by climatic conditions. Large-scale operations and small unit actions were equally affected. The influence of climate was felt in every effort of the German military establishment, whether on land, over water, or in the air.

Climate is a dynamic force in the Russian expanse; the key to successful military operations. He who recognizes and respects this force can overcome it; he who disregards or underestimates it is threatened with failure or destruction.

In 1941 the Wehrmacht did not recognize this force and was not prepared to withstand its effects. Crisis upon crisis and unnecessary suffering were the result. Only the ability of German soldiers to bear up under misfortune prevented disaster. But the German Army never recovered from the first hard blow.

Later the German armed forces understood the effects of climate and overcame them. That victory remained beyond reach was not due to climate alone, but in great measure to the fact that the German war potential was not equal to supporting a global war. The Wehrmacht was weakened by climatic conditions, and destroyed by the overpowering might of enemy armies.

WARFARE IN THE FAR NORTH

By General Der Infanterie Dr. Waldemar Erfurth
Wehrmacht Representative to Finnish Headquarters

Preface

Warfare in the Far North was prepared by Dr. Waldemar Erfurth at the EUCOM Historical Division Interrogation Inclosure, Neustadt, Germany, late in 1947. Dr. Erfurth represented the German Armed Forces High Command at Finnish Headquarters from June 1941 until the Finnish surrender in September 1944. He attained the rank of lieutenant general (General der Infanterie) in the German Army, and was a United States prisoner of war when this study was written.

Like all publications in the GERMAN REPORT SERIES, this is a translation from the German and presents the views of the German author without interpretation by American personnel. Throughout this pamphlet, Finnish and Russian combat methods, organization, and equipment are compared to those of the German Army. The descriptions of Finnish climate and terrain involve comparisons with that of Germany.

In the preparation of this revised edition, the German text has been retranslated, and certain changes in typography and chapter titles have been made to improve clarity and facilitate its use. The author's views, whatever they may be, find the same expression in the following translation as they do in the original German.

Those interested in a detailed history of the war in Finland, especially its political and diplomatic aspects, are referred to Dr. Erfurth's book Der Finnische Krieg 1941–1944 (Wiesbaden, 1950). No English translation is available at this time.

Department of the Army October 1951

The Climate
I. GERMAN IGNORANCE OF THE ARCTIC
The features peculiar to the theater of operations in the far north of Europe have given the recent wars in the Finnish area a character all their own. Terrain and climate always have a decisive influence on warfare. The tactical rules which had been worked out on the basis of experiences in central European theaters of war and which are adapted to normal conditions were applicable only to a limited extent in the cases of Karelia[1] and Lapland. In many respects warfare in the arctic follows rules of its own. The German High Command did not realize this fact until after the war was in progress. The German troops which were sent to Finland during World War II were not prepared for the special difficulties they encountered in combat in that trackless wilderness, in the endless virgin forests, and during the long arctic night. Only after paying dearly for their experiences did they become adjusted to the requirements of that theater. In the year 1941 Germany had no practical knowledge concerning the effects of intense cold on men, animals, weapons, and motor vehicles. The men in Berlin were not certain in their minds as to which type of military clothing would offer the best protection against arctic cold. In the past the German General Staff had taken no interest in the history of wars in the north and east of Europe. No accounts of the wars of Russia against the Swedes, Finns, and Poles had ever been published in German. Nobody had ever taken into account the possibility that some day German divisions would have to fight and to winter in northern Karelia and on the Murmansk coast. The German General Staff was inclined on the whole to limit its studies to the central European region. Only a few men (for instance, Baron von der Goltz, Count von Schlieffen, Baron von Freytag-Loringhofen) had

---

1 Karelia is a somewhat vague regional designation that applies to the area north and west of Lake Ladoga and west and south of the White Sea. The area was roughly bisected by the old (pre-1939) Russo-Finnish frontier, but most of it is now within the Karelo-Finnish Republic of the U.S.S.R.

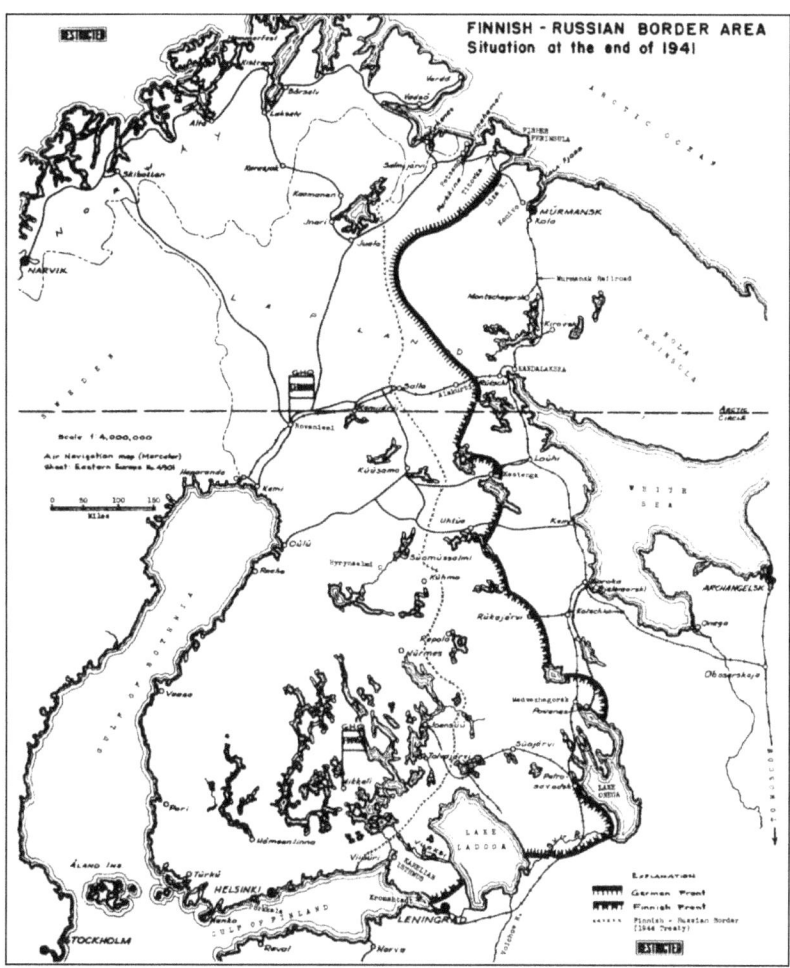

FINNISH - RUSSIAN BORDER AREA Situation at the end of 1941

attempted to have a larger area covered in the study program of General Staff officers. However, in so doing, they had encountered the opposition of the older generation which had been brought up in the tradition of von Moltke and which considered it sufficient to study the countries immediately surrounding Germany. In the absence of any stimulation on the part of the leaders of Germany's foreign policy toward more extensive studies, the northern regions of Europe remained practically unknown to the German soldier. From the days of Count von Schlieffen to the year 1940, the German General Staff in its studies on strategic concentrations had no longer concerned itself with the problem of an offensive campaign into Russia. The fact that the German soldier, finding himself involved quite suddenly in an offensive against the Murmansk railroad, was able after a certain period of adjustment to accustom himself to the peculiarities of the theater and make the best of the difficult conditions encountered in that type of warfare is proof of the great adaptability of the German soldier and is deserving of highest recognition. The Finns and the Russians were thoroughly familiar with the organization, clothing, equipment, armament, and troop training methods best suited for the theater situated between the Gulf of Finland and the Arctic Ocean, as well as with the most suitable tactics to be employed. Both are good and tough soldiers, knowing by sure instinct what has to be done in this terrain and climate. When the German soldier first came to the arctic, he was a tenderfoot, but by following the example of his Finnish brother-in-arms he reduced the differences between himself .and his model with comparative speed.

Because of the valuable qualities of the Finnish soldier, all German commanders on the Finnish-German front tried to have Finnish units attached to them whenever independent missions were assigned to the German units. How long Mannerheim wrangled with General Dietl at the beginning of the year 1943 about the return of the four Finnish battalions which had remained under the command of the German Twentieth Mountain Army! The endless Karelian forests had a discomforting, indeed a downright sinister, effect upon the German soldiers, many of whom had been raised in cities. They were depressed by the apparent limitlessness of the woods. On the other hand, the Finn who had grown up in the forests did not even notice the difficulties which made life hard for the German soldiers and, moreover, always knew how to act and what to do. After the heavy fighting of the summer and fall of 1941 in the Suojaervi area, near Kestenga, near Salla, and on the Liza, during which the German divisions suffered considerable losses without reaching their objective, the morale of some of the German troops had lowered noticeably. The realization that the prospects of going on furlough to Germany were becoming steadily poorer because of the crisis affecting the Finnish railroads and the freezing-over of the Baltic Sea had a depressing influence upon the German troops. Since the mail service became increasingly slower and more irregular because of winter weather conditions, a feeling of isolation was spreading among the soldiers. During that period German officers would occasionally make remarks more or less as follows: 'The German soldier is anxious to leave these never-ending Karelian woods; with half the losses, the Finns will accomplish twice as much here as the Germans.'

Correctly interpreting this situation, the German Army High Command turned in the fall of 1941 to Finnish General Headquarters for assistance. This was willingly and generously granted by Marshal Mannerheim. Beginning in the winter of 1941-42, courses in winter warfare of approximately twenty days' duration took place regularly in Finland. The Finns provided the instructor personnel, the school troops, and the school facilities for these courses. The students (mostly officers, but also some noncommissioned officers) were taken from the German eastern front. The instruction courses were held at several places in southern Finland: at the Kankaanpaa troop training center near Pori, at Camp Parola near Haemeenlinna, and in the Tuusola Civic Guard School near Helsinki. The German troop training center at Gross-Born was utilized on only one occasion when, owing to the freezing of the Baltic Sea in the beginning of 1942, it was impossible to move the Germans participating in these courses to Finland by boat. In this one instance the Finnish instructors were taken to Germany by airplane.

In the beginning the purpose of these courses was training in winter warfare, since the particularly hard winter of 1941-42 had caused considerable losses and critical reverses on the German eastern front. When the Germans requested that these courses be continued also in the summer in order to make the greatest possible number of German officers acquainted with the Finnish theater of war, the curriculum was extended to include training in combat in woods. During these courses, Finnish instructors with Finnish school troops at their disposal trained German regimental and battalion commanders in the command of these units in the dense forest. Also younger officers were trained in the conduct of combat patrols and long-range reconnaissance missions. Moreover, courses in long-distance skiing were held during the cold season.

These courses took into account that the largest part of Finland and the bordering regions to the east, as well as the northern part of Russia, constitute continuous wooded regions which are for the most part completely unexplored, and that the northern winter, of a severity to which the central European is not accustomed (deep snow, all waterways solidly frozen, very low temperatures, long nights), lasts through the greater part of the year.

II. PROTECTIVE MEASURES OF THE FINNS

The Finn, who learns to use an axe and a saw from childhood on, was able to make use of the means available in the woods and to spend the night in the open even in the most severe cold. The clothing of the Finnish soldier (fur cap with ear and neck protector, warm underwear, woolen scarf, fur gloves, warm footgear[2]) offered good protection against the cold. The Finnish tents, which were made of plywood and could be heated, proved to be very satisfactory. They could be put up quickly and moved easily. In wintertime these tents were set up for even a rest of but a few hours. When tents could not be set up, the Finnish

---

2 In wintertime the Finnish soldier wears boots of a larger size than in summertime so that he can wear two pairs of woolen socks.

troops built log fires and windbreaks in the open very rapidly. Whenever a pause of several days occurred during an advance, barrack-like huts were constructed with amazing speed. These offered protection against the cold and, in case the troops stayed in the same place for some time, were improved until they were quite comfortable. Thanks to the background and appropriate training of the troops, frostbite was practically unknown among the Finnish soldiers. In December 1941, when news reached Finland about the heavy losses the German Army was suffering in Russia because of the severe winter, Marshal Mannerheim made the following remarks on the subject: 'Losses among the troops because of frost weigh heavier on the commander's conscience than battle casualties. Because in this case there always remains the disturbing feeling that losses due to the cold might possibly have been avoided if greater precautions had been taken.'

The Finnish Supreme Commander could not understand why the High Command of the German Armed Forces and the Army administrative agencies had not made greater efforts in proper season to increase the German Army's ability to withstand the arduous Russian winter. The impression which Mannerheim, in his capacity as a general of the Czarist Army, had gained of German soldiers on the, Russian front in the First World War had given him a high respect for the careful and timely planning of the administrative agencies of the German Army. All the less could he understand the crisis which materialized in the winter of 1941-42 on the German eastern front, especially since he was not aware of the causes which had brought it about, such as, for example, the insufficient transport capacity of the railroads.

On the Finnish front, too, during the first year of joint warfare, many difficulties arose among the German troops which had an unfavorable effect upon the course of the war in the year 1941. However, the arctic climate was not the only peculiarity of the northern theater of war which made life hard for the German soldier. In comparison with the unhappy experiences of the German forces in Russia which resulted from the sudden beginning of winter, the German Army in Lapland was actually able to adjust itself to the requirements of the climate in the Far North with comparative speed and without great losses. The troops were able to cope in a surprisingly efficient manner with the inclemencies of the weather, the great variations in temperature (ranging from 950 F. in the summer to -400 F. in the winter), the heavy snowstorms, the long polar night, and the constant daylight in the summer. The ability of the German soldier to adjust to conditions on the Lapland front was enhanced by the facts that (a) the change-over from offensive to defensive in the fall of 1941 had been executed at such an early date that the construction of fortifications had progressed sufficiently by the time winter started; (b) there was an abundance of wood in the Karelian forests; and (c) supplies from Germany (winter clothing, warm quilted trousers, quilted blouses with hoods, snow shirts, a second blanket for every man, and good rations rich in vitamins) reached the troops on time despite the transportation crisis which materialized in Finland during the winter of 1941-42. There were difficulties only in the Murmansk sector, where the construction of fortified winter quarters in the rocky subsoil of the tundra was extremely difficult. Moreover, it was necessary to bring the required wood from great distances to the treeless coast of the Arctic Ocean. This instance once more proved the absolute necessity of making intensive and timely preparations for winter in the Far North. Nevertheless, it may be said that once the German troops became acclimated to Lapland their physical condition was and continued to be entirely satisfactory.

The Terrain
I. GENERAL CHARACTERISTICS
The peculiarities of the Finnish theater of war that caused the greatest combat difficulties were the absolute lack of roads and

the close character of the terrain which, with its vast zone of virgin forests, is so very different from the European landscape in latitudes farther south. The Karelian woods are under no forestry management such as is commonly applied in central Europe. The primeval forest is the result of natural reseeding. Old and young stands of trees are intermingled and frequently give rise to impenetrable thickets. This boundless forest is virtually unexplored. Throughout the trackless, desolate region deepest solitude and deathly silence reign supreme. Lakes, swamps, moors, and loose rock are characteristic of the Karelian landscape. Although on the Karelian Isthmus (the corridor between the Gulf of Finland and Lake Ladoga) and in the area between Lake Ladoga and Lake Onega the woods in some places are very dense and include old stands of trees, the timber becomes lighter and weaker the farther one goes north, until at last only scattered trees and bushes extend upward from an inextricable tangle of large rocks. In the Far North, rocky ground covered with reindeer moss, lichens, and blueberry, cranberry, and juniper bushes predominates in the wilderness. In the part of Karelia between Lake Onega and the White Sea, the tree line is about five hundred feet above sea level. 'Birches grow on the slopes between the conifer covered dales and the bare tops of the mountains, which are less than a thousand feet high. The conifers disappear completely north of the Arctic Circle. This is a· favorable region for birch forests, so characteristic of Lapland, with their short trunks often branching out like bushes. In the Petsamo region the completely treeless tundra extends up to the coast, where it changes into bare shingle along the Arctic Ocean.

This is an heroic landscape which has remained completely untouched by modern civilization. Since the dim past little or nothing has changed there. As in those days of long ago described in the songs of the Finnish epic, the 'Kalevala,' the hunter and fisher, the Lapp nomad with his reindeer herds, the individual loving solitude lives in the primeval wilderness, constantly struggling with the forces of nature.

II. EFFECT UPON OPERATIONS

Experiences gained during the Finnish-Soviet Winter War of 1939-40 had furnished certain definite indications for the conduct of operations in Karelia and Lapland. The course of this war had taught the following lessons:

1. The natural conditions along the frontier between Finland and the Soviet Union, the extremely extensive, pathless wasteland of the frontier region, the uneven terrain covered with loose rock and consequently passable only with difficulty, and the negligible development of roads are not suited to operations with large masses of troops of low mobility. Over broad stretches of country it is in many cases impossible to conduct operations involving large organizations, and in some instances it is pointless.

2. From the strategic point .of view the importance of the different sectors of the frontier region varies widely. Gain or loss of areas far removed from any kind of communication is of no decisive importance to the further course of war.

3. The characteristics of terrain and climate in the Far North are such that winter is the more favorable season for offensive campaigns, while summer is more suitable for defensive operations. Early and late winter are particularly favorable for attack operations; mid-winter with its deep snow is a less appropriate time for offensive warfare.

4. The transitions from winter to summer and from summer to winter constitute the muddy periods when use of the roads temporarily ceases or is greatly limited. The muddy period in the fall does not last as long as that in the spring. Because of the hard granitic soil of Finland and Russian Karelia, the roads usually dry out much quicker there than in southern Russia. In the Far North the principal concern is the melting of the snow which has fallen during the winter. The Finns have great experience and have developed special techniques

(snowplows, road-graders, etc.) to keep the main highways free from snow and open throughout the winter for the use of mail trucks and buses. The effect of brief periods of rain, which in Russia proper turn the roads into a hopeless condition, is negligible in Finland and the border area. During the muddy season, especially in the spring, there is no chance for effective air support because it is impossible for units of any considerable size to take off from the completely flooded airfields. Provisions were made to maintain flying operations on a limited scale through installation of latticed wooden runways. In these cases it was necessary to park the airplanes either on the runways or in their immediate vicinity. Such a procedure cannot be applied for organizations of any considerable size unless one accepts the necessity of expending enormous amounts of material and labor in the construction of latticed wooden runways and taxiing strips to the hardstands. Since both opponents were faced by identical conditions, air force activity, with only a few exceptions, was almost completely suspended on both sides during the muddy season.

The period between the Winter War of 1939-40[3] and the outbreak of the Finnish War against Russia in June 1941 was too short and the German Armed Forces High Command was too involved in other problems at that time to make possible the application of Finnish experiences to the advantage of the German troops. It was soon realized though that the horse-drawn and the motorized organizations of the German Army and the Waffen-SS which had been sent to Finland were too cumbersome. The Finnish Army, highly mobile both in summer and in winter because of its economical but very appropriate organization, would have been a good model for a suitable reorganization of the German troops operating in Finland. Fortunately, Dietl's mountain corps, which had been brought from northern Norway

---

3 The Winter War began 30 November 1939 and ended 13 March 1940.

and assigned the missions first of occupying the Petsamo area and later of attacking in the direction of Murmansk, was equipped with pack animals like all German mountain troops. Even though the Karelian area certainly cannot be considered as mountainous terrain, this type of organization proved very satisfactory since the pack animals were able to proceed off the roads and were not susceptible to the cold. As a consequence, during the later' course of the war the German organizations selected for duty in Finland consisted preferably of mountain troops. Nevertheless, it should be pointed out that even the trains of the mountain troops were much too bulky and cumbersome for the conditions prevailing in Finland,

During the Winter War the Finns gained experience in defensive operations conducted during the season of the year least suited for such operations. In World War II[4] Finnish and German troops took the offensive at the beginning of July 1941 along the long front between the Gulf of Finland and the Arctic Ocean. Not only during this war of movement but also throughout the entire duration of the immediately ensuing war of position, all operations in the Finnish theater in World War II took place in the same regions as did the Winter War. This facilitated the collection of certain experiences gained during both wars. The Winter War experiences of the Finnish Army were fully confirmed during World War II.

III. INDIVIDUAL SECTORS

In both wars the attackers as well as the defenders concentrated their main forces on the Karelian Isthmus and in the area northeast of Lake Ladoga. There never were any doubts or differences of opinion at Finnish General Headquarters about the strategic importance of the Karelian Isthmus and its suitability for the operations of strong forces. The road net in that region is well developed and in good repair so that operations by strong forces can be carried out on the Karelian

---
4 Finland declared war on Russia on 26 June 1941 and sued for peace on 19 September 1944.

Isthmus in both summer and winter.

The terrain estimate of the area northeast of Lake Ladoga was not quite so clear to the Finns. During the Winter War comparatively weak Finnish forces by bold counterattacks stopped the advance of the Red Army immediately northeast of Lake Ladoga and in the wooded and lake area of Tolvajaervi. The German Army High Command wanted the main body of the Finnish forces to advance in this region in the summer of 1941. The Finns, however, felt that the number and condition of the roads in Russian Karelia northeast of Lake Ladoga would be inadequate for the advance and the supply of troops in any considerable numbers. This view proved to be erroneous in the course of the Finnish summer offensive in the direction of the Svir and Petrosavodsk. Very soon there was a lack of divisions rather than roads. Additional forces had to be brought by rail from the Karelian Isthmus, where they could be spared, to the region northeast of Lake Ladoga. Thanks to this most timely reinforcement, the objective of the Finnish offensive towards the Svir was reached in a swift operation. Farther north on the Finnish eastern border, Finnish and German troops pressed forward on the same roads over which the Red Army had invaded Finland during the Winter War. The following are the roads which run from the Murmansk railroad in the direction of the Finnish border and which were used by the Finns and the Germans:

1. The Kotshkoma–Rukajaervi road, the continuation of which via Repola toward Nurmes or Kuhmo had been inadequate for the Finns for moving troops and supplies in the year 1941. This inadequacy made it necessary to build a parallel military road for rather long distances.
2. The Kem–Uhtua–Suomussalmi road.
3. The Louhi–Kestenga–Kuusamo road (this road had been spared by the Russians in the Winter War).
4. The Kandalaksha–Alakurti–Salla–Kemijaervi road.

5. The "Russian" road along the arctic coast, which had been built after the Moscow Treaty of 1940 from Konivo on the Kola Fjord via Titovka up to the Finnish border and which from the summer of 1941 had been improved in the zone of the German troops. (The Russian Winter War invasion in the Petsamo region did not come from Murmansk but from the Fisher Peninsula.)

Out of this arose the well-known World War II designations of sectors:[5]

1. Rukajaervi (Kotshkoma),
2. Uhtua (Kern),
3. Kestenga (Louhi),
4. Salla (Kandalaksha), and
5. Petsamo (Murmansk).

The regions between these sectors, entirely remote from any traffic, remained completely untouched by the war. No attempt was made by either side to penetrate deeper into the vast, trackless wastes of the border marshes. After the war of movement had given way to position warfare, Russian partisan detachments and Finnish Sissi[6] patrols attempted at times to encircle the flank of one sector or another in order to interrupt the flow of supplies or to rouse the sparse population of the border zone. But these undertakings only bore the stamp of minor warfare and were of no consequence to the main task.

IV. SIGNIFICANCE OF THE MURMANSK RAILROAD

The Murmansk railroad played a very special role in World War II. It was the most important strategic objective for the Finns and Germans; only by seizing it could the Soviet Union be cut off from supplies coming from the U.S.A. and Great Britain over the shortest route by way of the Arctic Ocean.

The fight for the Murmansk railroad disclosed the undeniable

---

[5] The designation was derived mostly from the main locality in the German-Finnish zone, sometimes also from the objective on the Murmansk railroad (designated in parentheses).

[6] Detachments composed of border population familiar with conditions in the wilderness.

superiority of the Red Army over the Germans and Finns in the realm of transportation. The fact that all offensive plans of the Finns and the Germans came to naught in the region between Lake Onega and the Arctic Ocean can be traced in the last analysis to the existence of the railroad and its undisturbed operation by the Russians. The importance of this fact warrants our taking a look at the transportation situation in the Russo-Finnish border region.

The railroad from Petrosavodsk to Murmansk was built during World War I and was a continuation of the Leningrad-Petrosavodsk line constructed back in 1899. As the means of communication with the only ice-free Russian harbor on the Murmansk coast, it was not only of great importance in marine commerce but also in a war against Finland it assured the Red Army of a great strategic superiority over its Finnish neighbor. Primarily, it enabled the Russian Army to assemble and shift troops rapidly along the eastern frontiers of Finland. The automobile road from Rovaniemi to Petsamo (the so-called Arctic Highway), built by the Finns and completed in 1929, had promoted tourist traffic to Finnish Lapland, but for military transportation it could not compare at all with the capacity of the Murmansk railroad. The northernmost Finnish railroad running from Kemi (on the Gulf of Bothnia) via Rovaniemi to Kemijaervi was the least efficient of the Finnish railroads.

The efficiency of the Murmansk railroad during the last war was estimated as follows: The railroad bed was not good and repairs were often necessary. But the Russians had the required personnel and materiel ready at numerous points for rapid repairs. The average speed of the trains was 20–25 miles per hour. The Leningrad–Petrosavodsk line was double-tracked. At the time of the Finnish surrender (1944) the intended double-tracking of the rest of the line had not yet been carried out. The average daily traffic on the Soroka–Kandalaksha line in the summer of 1942 amounted to 10–15 trains in two sections in both directions. An increase up to 40 trains in two sections daily is alleged to have been possible. Bituminous coal was the fuel generally used for the locomotives. In 1939 the line was electrified from Kandalaksha to Murmansk. The average speed on this stretch is said to have been 40 miles per hour.

By the laying of a new single-track railroad in 1938–41 from Soroka via the region south of the White Sea to Oboserskaya (on the Archangelsk–Moscow railroad), the Murmansk railroad was connected with the Archangelsk railroad and thereby to the railroad net of inner Russia, greatly increasing its strategic possibilities. When enemy action impeded railroad traffic at any point along the Leningrad-Sodoka line, the front in the Far North up to the arctic coast could always be supplied by making use of the new Oboserskaya–Soroka railroad. That was the case, for example, in the summer of 1941, after the Finns had first cut the Murmansk railroad at the Svir River, and later had taken possession of the entire line from the Svir via Petrosavodsk to Medvezhegorsk and beyond. The supply of the Soviet front in the Far North as well as Anglo-American lend-lease shipments to Russia remained completely undisturbed by the loss of the southern portion of the Murmansk railroad.

As far as is known the Finnish-German offensive of 1941 at no point reached its objective—the vital northern stretch of the Murmansk railroad. Soviet resistance could not be broken despite repeated attempts; but the Red Army, which eventually passed to the offensive, did not fare much better. In stubborn and costly fighting the most that could be gained was small improvements of position, but at no point was a decisive success achieved.

After the Germans and Finns had failed to gain possession of the Murmansk railway in 1941, and after Operation LACHSFANG[7] (Salmon Catch) of 1942 had to be abandoned as

---

7 LACHSFANG was an elaborate plan for a junction of the Finns and German Army Group North in the area southeast of Lake Ladoga.

too ambitious, other means were tried to reach the same objective. All the expedients which were employed, namely, bombing of railroad bridges and viaducts by the Luftwaffe, frequent air attacks on Murmansk and other railroad stations, and demolitions by combat patrols or by parachuted commando troops, led to no lasting result. Only slight damage was ever inflicted. This the Russians were able to repair after a few hours' work. The strategic problem—the destruction of the railroad either completely or for a long time—was never solved.

V. THE FINNISH TRANSPORTATION NETWORK

The transportation situation of the Finns was quite critical during the war. The Finnish Chief of Transportation, Colonel (later General) Roos, was an outstanding specialist in the field of transportation. He did what was possible; nevertheless, serious crises arose, especially at the end of 1941.

All personnel and the bulk of the freight transported to and from Finland moved over the Baltic Sea. The German army in Lapland was supplied for the most part by water via Kirkenes and Liinahamari. Lesser quantities went via the Baltic Sea, the Finnish railroad, and then overland by the Arctic Highway. A small portion of supplies to the front, evacuation to the rear, and small numbers of replacements went via Sweden.

Transport by water via the Baltic was seriously curtailed and delayed by Russian U-boats, mines, the necessity of convoys, shortage of tonnage, lack of buoys, inadequate storage facilities in the Finnish harbors, and shortage of unloading personnel. From the middle of January the Baltic Sea freezes for a rather long period, so that shipping stops altogether at this time of the year.

Railroad transportation in Finland suffered not only from shortage of rolling stock (a result of the expansion of the railroad system and of the increasing demands made by the war) but also from the low and differing capacities of lines and stations, the lack of shunting yards and of sufficient Finnish railroad personnel, as well as from delays in the unloading of cars, the effects of the cold upon woodburning engines, and partisan activity.

The German Army command was able to deliver some serviceable broad-gauge rolling stock captured from the Russians. On the other hand, Finnish requests for the construction of new railroad equipment in Germany could not be met.

The northern line from Rovaniemi to the front was a special headache to the Finnish and German railroad authorities. The line was originally intended to handle the traffic of the primitive economy of a thinly populated and self-sufficient region. The Finns worked on this line continually during the entire duration of the war to increase its capacity. The section from Oulu via Kemi to Rovaniemi had been improved. To relieve pressure on the northern line, the Twentieth Mountain Army with its own labor force and material built the Hyrynsalmi-Kuusamo field railroad, about 200 miles long. The work, which was to facilitate the supply of the right flank corps of the Twentieth Mountain Army (at first the Finnish III Corps, later the German XVIII Corps), was considerably delayed because of lack of skilled labor and because the difficulties of building the railroad had been underestimated.

The German and Finnish troop trains always moved over Finnish railroads quickly and smoothly. The Finnish railroad personnel showed itself resourceful and very skillful in improvising. German soldiers on furlough went through Turku in the summer and via Hanko in winter. The bottleneck was not in railroad transportation but in sea transport. Russian U-boats, mines, lack of shipping, and other things caused this bottleneck. A monthly average of about 25,000 Germans on furlough was carried to and from the Reich.

Despite all improvements and expedients, the capacity of the Finnish railroads imposed a limit on any large-scale increase in the number of German troops located in Lapland, a limit which could not be exceeded because of the problems incidental to supplying the troops. To be sure, under favorable weather conditions and during the long days of the arctic summer the Finnish railroad authorities were able to get more out of the low-capacity northern line for an operation of brief duration. An increase in the number of troops and especially horses would have led to reductions in the level of supplies on the German front in Lapland. Railroad construction troops and material would have to be assembled in advance of any extensive and lengthy operation in order to first build the lines that would be required. Only with considerable German help would this have been possible.

Oversea transportation to and from Finland was considerably interfered with by enemy action during the war. Besides a total loss of Finnish and German shipping sunk in the Baltic, ships repeatedly ran aground because there were no buoys. These ships were then laid up for lengthy periods. Ships had to be used as escort vessels for convoys because of the presence of Russian naval vessels based at Kronshtadt and Leningrad. This resulted in loss of their services as transport or supply ships. It was unfortunate that the German-Finnish offensive of 1941 did not succeed in permanently knocking out the Soviet naval bases.

Organization and Tactics

The course of the fighting for the Murmansk railroad confirmed the lessons of the Winter War and seemed to justify the following conclusions.:

1. Warfare in primeval wilderness and in the tundra is tied to the few available roads. This is especially true in the summer. When the situation required an encircling movement off the road in the border area, time-consuming road construction work became a prerequisite, requiring not days but weeks. Decisions once made could not be reconsidered. Once troops

had started advancing through the wilderness or once the order had been given committing them, nothing could be changed. The movement had to run to its completion. Everything required endless time to bring results.

2. The most favorable season of the year for a war of movement in high latitudes is the winter. The attempt to reach the Murmansk railroad would perhaps have been successful if it had been undertaken, as Mannerheim had suggested, at the beginning of March and with sufficient forces. In the Far North the winter roads play an important role. Running over the ice of lakes and moors, they are the nature-given traffic communications in the long winter. The winter road over the ice of Lake Ladoga played an especially important role during the war; over it went the supplies for besieged Leningrad and the evacuation of a considerable portion of the Leningrad population. Neither the Germans nor the Finns were able to interfere with these movements. Overland communication in Finland for seven to eight months of the year takes place by sleigh, the method preferred for use in winter on the snow-covered ice. The ice covering usually does not melt until June, which is later than the snow thaws on land roads.

I. SKI TROOPS

During early and late winter, troops equipped with skis and akjas can operate off the roads and bring along all that is really needed for existence and for combat; but they must leave behind everything that cannot be carried easily through primeval forest or rocky wilderness. The superior skill of the Finnish troops in covering long distances gave them a high mobility and consequently a decided ascendency over troops of the Red Army in the Winter War. The Soviet command recognized the great importance of using skis in fighting in the Far North. According to Finnish accounts, the Russians formed and trained special elite ski units in Siberia and concentrated them before World War II on the eastern border of Finland. These Soviet troops soon acquired great skill and during the war became almost as good as the Finnish ski units, whose marching speed is surprisingly great even in especially difficult terrain. Combat operations, even in trackless regions, are executed much faster on skis in winter than on foot in summer. The open Banks of the Finnish-German sectors between Lake Onega and the Arctic Ocean could only be effectively protected by mobile Finnish ski patrol detachments. The fight against the Soviet partisans was carried on by the Finns with the passion of skilled and experienced hunters. It was most successful in winter when the enemy's tracks could be followed in the snow, and he could be brought to bay.

The strength of the Finnish soldier lies in individual combat. The Finns possess an infallible instinct for finding their way in the dense growth of the pathless wilds. They are accurate trail readers and move noiselessly in the woods. Nothing is heard or seen of Finnish troops whether resting or marching, even from the closest proximity. Terrain training is of a very high order. A special technique for movement through woods has been developed and practiced so that the troops advance quickly, in the right direction and without losing contact. A Finnish company moves in the primeval forest just as smoothly and unerringly as a German company in the open landscape of central Europe. All Finns are enthusiastic hunters and sport lovers and fighting wakens in them all their hunting instincts. The aggressiveness of the troops is very keen. Their achievements in long-range combat patrolling cannot be surpassed.

II. ORGANIZATION OF FINNISH TROOP UNITS

The Finnish infantry is equipped with skis in winter. Accustomed from earliest infancy to move on skis during over half of the year, the Finn accomplishes marvels in covering long distances. The use of the simple Finnish toe-binding enables the soldier to put on and take off his skis quickly. The enemy is approached on skis in small, well-separated groups echeloned in depth. The crouching skiers, camouflaged in snow shirts, rapidly approach the enemy in short bounds. Just before the final rush they quickly kick off their skis. Often the men drag their skis along, or else a member of the group gathers all the skis and brings them forward.

The Finnish cavalry in general has the mission of mounted infantry. The guiding principle in its training stresses encirclement and attack deep in the enemy Bank. It is able to carry out this task because the Finnish horse is used to traveling even over difficult wooded terrain covered with rocky debris. In the winter the cavalry troops are also equipped with skis.

Training and organization of the Finnish artillery is primarily designed for combat in woods and achieved a high level of efficiency during the last war, despite the fact that the armament was to some extent old-fashioned and lacked uniformity. Since opportunities for observation were limited in the wilderness each battery, as a rule, needed several observation posts. Therefore, every battery had at least two forward observers. By means of a signal-communication net specially organized for this purpose, every forward observer was able to deliver fire with all batteries of the regiment. In the defense it was even possible to deliver fire with all medium and heavy mortars. The forward observers of the mortars in turn were able to do the same. The forward observers were connected with the firing positions by wire and radio. Great stress was laid on surprise fires. Survey was well perfected and very rapid when the aiming circle was employed.

In tank combat the Finns lacked practical experience. Not until World War II did the Finns undertake to organize an armored division. The materiel consisted of captured Russian equipment, to which a few German tanks were added in the last year of the war. Training was based on German regulations. The Karelian Isthmus is especially favorable for armored operations.

The Russians employed numerous tank units there in the Winter War and in the summer of 1944. But tanks were also used in the Red Army's offensive on the Svir in April 1942.

On the long Finnish east front no tanks were used up to the time of the Finnish capitulation. When the Russians advanced against the Petsamo region in October 1944, the Red Army reportedly used only a few tanks against the German front. These weapons moved on the roads; undoubtedly tanks would encounter great difficulties on the rocky slopes of the tundra. In the Kandalaksha sector a Soviet tank unit advanced through the trackless wilderness and participated in the attack on the hilly country in the Salla area.

Finnish training of antitank units was hampered by lack of practical experience. Sufficient quantities of modern materiel were available by the end of the war.

The technical and tactical aspects of Finnish signal communications were still in the first stages of development. The use of bare wire, occasioned by special conditions of combat in woods and the critical situation in the manufacture of field signal cable, was remarkable. For this purpose a galvanized iron wire 2-mm. thick was strung overhead. In winter, if the situation was urgent, it was also possible to utilize the insulating property of completely dry snow by laying wire in the snow as a metallic circuit. Messenger dogs and carrier pigeons were not used in the Finnish Army.

III. FINNISH TRAINING DOCTRINE

The Finnish troops had been trained according to German principles and were in possession of the German training regulations. A comparatively large number of the senior Finnish officers had served with the 27th Prussian Light Infantry Battalion in their youth and had fought against Russia in the First World War. They were thoroughly familiar with the ideology of the German soldier. However, in a number of Finnish officers of high rank the influence of French principles of command was unmistakable. Some of the Finnish generals who held the highest posts in the last war had been detailed to the École de Guerre after World War I, and thus became acquainted with French doctrine. Perhaps this influence is responsible for the fact that many of the Finnish higher commanders remained farther behind their troops than the German commanders did in the last war. However, it is also possible that this difference in concept as to the place of the commander in battle resulted from the fact that the Finnish Army had been trained mainly for defensive warfare. It is evident that there was no one in Finland before the summer of 1941 who gave any thought to the possibility of a large-scale Finnish offensive against the Red Army.

IV. MARSHAL MANNERHEIM AS A COMMANDER

Marshal Mannerheim received his training as a soldier in the Imperial Russian Army and attained a high rank in it. He studied warfare under the most varied circumstances (in the Russo-Japanese War, World War I, the Finnish War for Freedom, the Winter War, and World War II) on the side of the Russians as well as on the side of their opponents. His wealth of experience, extensive intellectual culture, and outstanding traits of character destined him to find an undisputed place among the great military leaders of history. Characteristic of his art of strategy was his caution, based on the realization of his great responsibility. "I must be cautious," the Marshal once said to the German general in his headquarters, "because the Finnish Army is so small, the theater of war so gigantic, and the losses suffered thus far are so high." In typically Finnish fashion he loved to study things out and to deliberate before deciding on a course of action. But once he had made a decision, he carried it out energetically and unwaveringly. His authority in the Finnish Armed Forces was unlimited.

V. PECULIARITIES OF FINNISH TACTICS

For the first time in its existence the Finnish Army had the opportunity to prove its mettle in an offensive on a large scale during the summer of 1941. It performed its mission with the highest honor, at first east of Lake Ladoga, then on the Karelian Isthmus. On the long eastern boundary of Finland the offensive of the year 1941 soon lost the momentum and character of a large-scale battle and broke up into local actions fought by isolated combat groups. In this type of warfare the Finnish soldier felt at home and did excellent work. As the Winter War and World War II have shown, fighting in the lonely and trackless wilderness of eastern Finland must necessarily assume the character of guerilla warfare, in which the Finns are unsurpassed. Submachine guns, hand grenades, and the Finnish dagger (puukko) here played the chief roles.

Finnish tactics aim to penetrate the front of the enemy, to separate the enemy's strong points from each other, to cut off these strong points completely from all arteries of supply, and to encircle them. In this manner the famous "mottis" (a Finnish word with no English equivalent, which means an encircled enemy center of resistance) were formed in the Winter War. Here the fighting completely demonstrated the great superiority of the Finnish soldier over the Red Army man. In the Winter War the fighting for the mottis clearly represented an attempt to starve the enemy into surrender. This was so because the Finns had little heavy artillery with which to break the Russian resistance. During World War II, when the Finns were well equipped with German artillery and ammunition, the resistance of surrounded strong points was crushed much more quickly. The struggle for the mottis was always a very stubborn one and demanded the utmost in bravery. It ended either in victory or annihilation because the Russian soldier continued his stubborn resistance even if there was little prospect of success. He fought courageously until his destiny was fulfilled.

VI. RUSSIAN TACTICS IN THE FAR NORTH

The events of the Winter War created in many of the nations not participating in the struggle the impression that the Red Army with its crushing superiority in numbers and modern armament had accomplished much less than might have been expected. After a 100-day war characterized by bitter fighting, the situation of the Finns had become critical only on the Karelian Isthmus. On the entire eastern boundary of Finland the Soviet attack had been checked and repulsed with great losses for the Russians. To the Red Army man the Finnish soldier, insufficiently armed and lacking ammunition, had proved himself to be a superior fighter.

The achievements of the Red Army in the Winter War lagged far behind expectations. This resulted in an erroneous opinion even in Germany concerning the military worth of the Russians. It was a surprise when the Red Army in World War II accomplished so much more in Russia proper and showed a strength and hardiness not expected by the Germans. How can this disparity in the achievements of the Russians in the two wars in Finland be explained? On 4 March 1943 Mannerheim made the following remarks on this subject to the German general assigned to Finnish Headquarters:

"The Russians have learned a lot from you. Timoshenko himself said precisely that to our commissioners after the Winter War. This means that the Soviet generals are apt pupils and very quickly put into practice what they have learned. Today the commanders of the Red Army attack boldly and aggressively, and employ envelopment tactics just as the German generals do. In the Winter War of 1939–40 the poor showing of the Russians was not camouflage; it was the true picture. Since that time they have learned a great deal and made tremendous progress."

There can be no doubt today that the Red Army evaluated the experiences gained in the Winter War in a surprisingly short time. Another surprising thing is the fact that the Red Army did not lose its vigor during World War II, as so often happens in the course of a long conflict. Despite serious crises and enormous losses, the Red Army maintained its power of resistance and

A soldier in winter clothing adjusting a heavy mortar, Russia, January 1944.

attack and even improved in quality in several respects. This was due to its rapid adaptation of the technical developments of the period. Whatever the Soviet infantry lost in combat value was more than counterbalanced by the rapid increase of the tank arm.

The magnitude of this admirable achievement is without parallel in the history of wars and present day armies. However, because of the peculiar character of the north country, the Red Army was unable to assert its superiority over the Finns in the Winter War. After the Red Army had beaten off the Finnish-German offensive of the year 1941, it tried in the spring of 1942 to throw the enemy back by counterattacking on the Svir front, in the Kestenga sector, and on the coast of the Arctic Ocean. These attempts, based on the old methods, were just as unsuccessful and costly as the Soviet offensive of the Winter War against the eastern frontier of Finland and the attacks against the Murmansk railroad executed by the Germans and Finns in 1941. The experiences gained by both sides in these wars warrant the conclusion that the Karelian wilderness is not suitable for decisive operations on any large scale. The offensive attempts were not repeated by either side until the summer of 1944. In the long interim uneventful position warfare prevailed on the extensive front between the Gulf of Finland and the Arctic Ocean.

Then, on 10 June 1944 the offensive on the Karelian Isthmus, prepared by the Red Army on a large scale, began as a complete surprise to the Finns. The Russian attack was carried out according to the latest principles which had been developed in technical science and in the tactics of war. The Russian method of attack, so successfully applied against the German east front since the fall of 1942, namely, smashing a limited portion of a position by the combined attack of an immensely superior air force and massed artillery and then driving through the resulting gap with numerous tanks, led to rapid and complete success on the Karelian Isthmus. The Russian penetration widened with destructive speed to a break-through. The Finnish High Command quickly realized that it was impossible to regain the old positions by the committing of reserves. The only thing to be done was to withdraw the troops, while they were still able to fight, from the attacked sector to a secondary defense line where Finnish reinforcements brought up from sectors not under attack, and supporting troops and weapons provided by the German High Command, could join the withdrawing Finnish troops. This covering position was established in the Viipuri-Vuoksi area, where the Finnish Army previously had brought the assault of the Red Army to a halt during the Winter War. This position, which was only very hastily organized, had the advantage of being located in terrain which allowed the Russians to make only limited use of their offensive weapons. The main portion of the position lay in extensive wooded terrain which denied observation to the Red Air Force. Numerous lakes and the broad Vuoksi River assured comparative safety from tank attacks. The Soviet offensive came to a standstill at this Viipuri-Vuoksi position and never got started again.

After about a month the Russians definitely discontinued their offensive against the Finns and moved strong forces from the Karelian Isthmus to the region south of Leningrad, where the offensive of the Red Army against German Army Group North was making good progress. This decision of the Russians to shift their main effort may have been prompted by the consideration that it would be easier to gain successes opposite the German front, which had already been shaken, than opposite the Finnish Front, which had ' become stabilized. The Soviet Army High Command may have also been influenced in their decision to break off the offensive against the Finns by the very costly experience they had had in this area during the Winter War.

VII. LESSONS FROM THE RUSSIAN SUMMER OFFENSIVE

The course of the Soviet offensive north of Leningrad in the summer of 1944 led to the following conclusions:

1. The Karelian Isthmus is the most suitable area on the Finnish-Russian frontier for decisive operations of large-

sized units. Here the road and railroad nets permit the quick concentration of large forces for a large-scale attack in the territory between Lake Ladoga and the Gulf of Finland. (This confirms experiences of the Winter War.)
2. The Red Army's method of attack brought into play the great superiority of the Russians in numbers and modern means of combat. The Finnish positions, which had been well organized during a period of two and a half years, were quickly penetrated and rolled up in a violent assault. (Experiences from the Soviet offensives against the German east front confirm this.)
3. The large-scale Soviet attack in the summer of 1944 was, however, only initially successful. The Finns were able to bring it to a stand-still on the Viipuri–Vuoksi line and to drive it back eventually.

This Finnish victory was gained because of:

a. Mannerheim's early decision not to fight for the position when it was penetrated but to reorganize his forces on a secondary line.
b. The solidity of the Finnish soldier and the preservation of his inherent steadiness and fighting qualities despite reverses.
e. The timely German assistance with troops, planes, armor-piercing weapons, and ammunition.
d. The natural strength of the Viipuri–Vuoksi line.
e. The season of the year was favorable for defensive operations. It is probable that in winter the Viipuri–Vuoksi line would not have been able to check the enemy for any length of time.

Prospects

The capitulation formula dictated by the Soviet Government and accepted by the Finns in September 1944 again confirmed the cessions of territory which had been stipulated by the Peace of Moscow of 1940. The cession of the Karelian Isthmus, the country northeast and north of Lake Ladoga, and the hilly region of Salla was confirmed and, in addition, the region of Petsamo had to be ceded to the Russians. The leasehold of Hanko was given back to the Finns. On the other hand, Porkkala, which is located directly in front of the gates of Helsinki, became a Soviet strong point for the next fifty years.

These territorial changes alter the basis of all staff planning for warfare on the Finnish-Russian frontier and demand entirely new points of view on economic, military, and political matters. The axiom of Heraclitus that 'war is the father of all things' has again proved its validity in the fighting in high latitudes. The last Finnish war introduced a new chapter in the history of the earth. From now on the arctic region is accessible to man in both war and peace. The events of the wars in the Far North proved that even large numbers of men are able to live, work, and fight in the desolate regions north of the Arctic Circle. Modern technical science has provided the means for overcoming difficulties of climate and terrain in the frigid zone and has even made life tolerable there. The man of the 20th century has the means of pushing into the arctic region in rather large numbers, establishing healthy homes and places to work, and preserving the creative impulses and the joy of life of the pioneers in the Far North. Airmail and radio establish communication with the outer world. It was shown during the war that suitable organization can provide all the necessities for spending the winter in high latitudes. Today no real obstacles exist to opening up the 'arctic region. If strong incentives and a prospect of good returns exist, courageous and enterprising men will be attracted by the land of the midnight sun. The rich mineral treasures which lie buried in 'the earth at the northern cap of the globe will act as powerful incentives for penetrating the polar region. On the Kola Peninsula, in the Petsamo region, in northern Sweden, great treasures lie in the earth which are needed by the modern man of industry and will be exploited by him. Navigation is possible in the Arctic Ocean throughout the year. In order to avoid air and submarine attacks, most of the convoys from England and America to Murmansk and Archangelsk traveled during the dark winter months. When the Far North of Europe develops into an industrial region, the harbors on the Arctic Ocean (Murmansk, Liinahamari, Kirkenes, Narvik) will flourish. The shortest air route between the Old and the New World is via the North Pole. Therefore this will be an area of intense activity in the future, both in peace and in war. In this connection problems which arose during World War II in the fields of radio navigation and radar instruments still remain to be solved. The disturbances and deflections caused by the proximity of the magnetic pole will require exhaustive research. To this must be added the difficulties occasioned by the tremendous size and emptiness of the region which increase the difficulty of installing a sufficiently dense net of radio stations and radar instruments. It is in these fields that future development will present complicated problems, the solution of which, however, is already indicated.

The new boundary between the Soviet Union and Finland—Norway too has now become an immediate neighbor of the Soviet Union—creates a new strategic situation in the Far North. Karelia with its numerous waterways and lakes and its trackless wilderness no longer lies as a protective zone in front of Finland proper but has become a Russian troop concentration area. If there should be another armed settlement of differences in the European arctic region, the Soviet armies will stand immediately in front of the land regions most important to the defense of Finnish independence. This fact also makes Sweden's position much less secure than formerly. There is no doubt that the Russians, having the energy and flair for doing things in the big way characteristic of the Soviet Union, will immediately organize Karelia into a powerful base from which all Scandinavia could be held in subjection. Soon new branch railroads and military roads will be built from the Murmansk railroad through the Karelian wilderness in the direction of the new Finnish boundary. The chief objectives toward which Soviet endeavors point extend from Viipuri to Turku and the Aaland Islands, from Salla to Kemi and Oulu, and from Murmansk and Petsamo to Kirkenes. New forces have appeared in the arctic region. These territories are no longer at the end of the world far removed from human contacts. Who can say what the future has in store for the land of the midnight sun? Indications increasingly point to the growing importance of the polar regions for the future of mankind.

SMALL UNIT ACTIONS DURING THE RUSSIAN CAMPAIGN: COMPANY G

By General-Major Burkhart Mueiler-Hillebrand, General-Major Heilmuth Reinhardt, and others

Company G Counterattacks During a Snowstorm (November 1941)

This action is typical of the fighting in the late autumn of 1941, when Russian resistance began to stiffen west of Moscow and the ill-equipped German troops had to rally all their energy to continue the advance toward the Russian capital.

In November 1941 the 464th Infantry Regiment of the German 253d Infantry Division was occupying field fortifications about 60 miles northeast of Rzhev. On the regiment's right flank was Hill 747 (map below). Since the hill afforded an extensive view of the German rear area, the Russians had made repeated attempts to capture it in an effort to undermine the position of the 464th Infantry Regiment. The hill had changed hands several times, but was now occupied by the Germans. The presence of heavy weapons including assault guns, as well as reports of repeated reconnaissance thrusts, gave rise to the belief that the Russians were preparing for another attack against the hill. Accordingly, the regimental commander withdrew Company G from the sector it was holding and committed it on the regiment's right flank.

After reporting to battalion headquarters around noon on 15 November, Lieutenant Viehmann, the commander of Company G, accompanied by his platoon leaders, undertook a terrain reconnaissance. A heavy snowfall set in. As the group was returning from the reconnaissance mission, submachine gun and

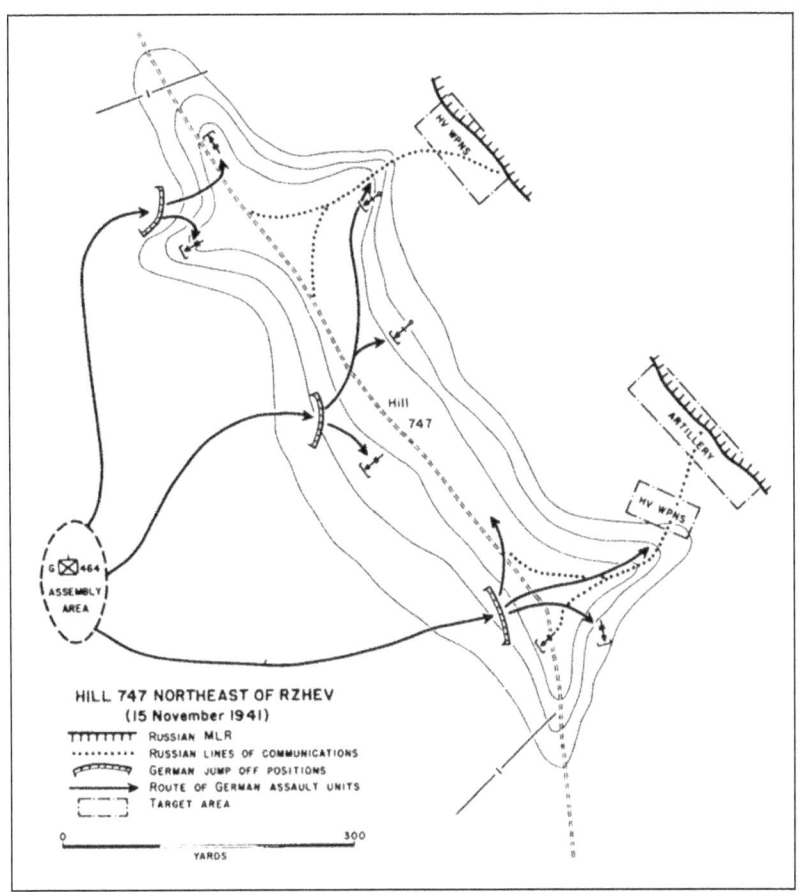

HILL 747 NORTHEAST OF RZHEV (15 November 1941)

mortar fire was heard from the direction of Hill 747. The company commander attached little importance to this at the time. However, upon arriving at the battalion CP he learned that the Russians had taken advantage of the snowstorm and had seized the hill without artillery or mortar support in a surprise raid. An immediate counterattack by German troops failed to dislodge the Russians.

Viehmann thereupon received orders to recapture the hill in a surprise attack to be launched at 2200. Regimental headquarters attached a medium mortar platoon and a light howitzer platoon to the company and promised artillery support.

Viehmann formed three assault parties and moved them into jumpoff positions close to the Russian line under cover of darkness. The infantry company to the right was to divert the attention of the defending force at the time of the actual attack, while the unit to the left was to support the attack with its fire. Artillery and heavy weapons were to open fire on specified areas at prearranged flare signals.

The German assault parties occupied their jumpoff positions without attracting the attention of the defending Russians. The party in the center, led by Viehmann, was only about 35 yards from the nearest Russian position. Close observation of the Russian defenses and the actions of individual soldiers indicated that a German attack was not anticipated. The Russian sentries were shivering from the cold and were by no means alert. Rations and supplies were being drawn. Not far from Viehmann's observation point a Russian detail was unloading furs and felt boots from a sled.

At 2200 the German assault parties, shouting loudly, broke into the Russian position. The attack confused the Russians, who dropped everything and attempted to make their way to the rear. Their escape, however, was prevented by the two assault parties that, at the beginning of the attack, had skirted either side of the hill and severed the Russian lines of communications. Unaware of the fighting, the Russian heavy weapons and artillery remained silent throughout the attack. When the signal flare went up, the German artillery and heavy weapons opened fire, laying a barrage on the Russian-held side of the hill. Two Russian machineguns covering each flank put up fierce resistance before being silenced in the hand-to-hand fighting.

After 45 minutes Hill 747 was completely in the hands of the Germans; their former MLR had been reoccupied and communications established with adjacent units. About 60 prisoners, 7 medium mortars, 5 heavy machineguns, 3 antitank guns, and large quantities of ammunition were taken. In the morning 70 Russian dead were found on the hill. Of the five German casualties, only one was severely wounded.

The manner in which the Russians exploited the snowstorm in carrying out a surprise attack without artillery or mortar support was typical of Russian infantry combat methods in wintertime.

The Russians launched their attack before winter clothing had been issued; some of the men wore only thin summer uniforms. As a stimulant, each Russian soldier was issued five tablets which had an effect similar to that of alcohol and a large ration of sugar cubes. In addition, the men were promised a special liquor ration upon completion of their mission. The sugar and tablets were presumably issued to counteract the discomfort caused by the temperature of 16° F. However, once the effects of these stimulants wore off, the men began to feel the cold acutely and their senses became numbed, as was observed in the case of the Russian sentries. During the German assault to retake Hill 747 the Russian defenders appeared to be as susceptible to the cold as were the Germans. This must be considered an isolated case, however, since the Russian soldiers were generally able to endure extremely low temperature. At the same time it indicates that some of the Russian units were insufficiently prepared for winter combat and had to improvise protective measures to overcome the rigors of the unexpectedly early winter weather.

Company G Operates in Deep Snow (January 1942)

On 13 January Company G of the 464th Infantry Regiment was ordered to provide protection against Russian partisan raids on the division's supply line, which led from Toropets via Village M to Village O (map overleaf). To this end the company was reinforced by two heavy machineguns, two 80-mm. mortars, and one antitank platoon.

On the evening of 14 January the company, mounted in

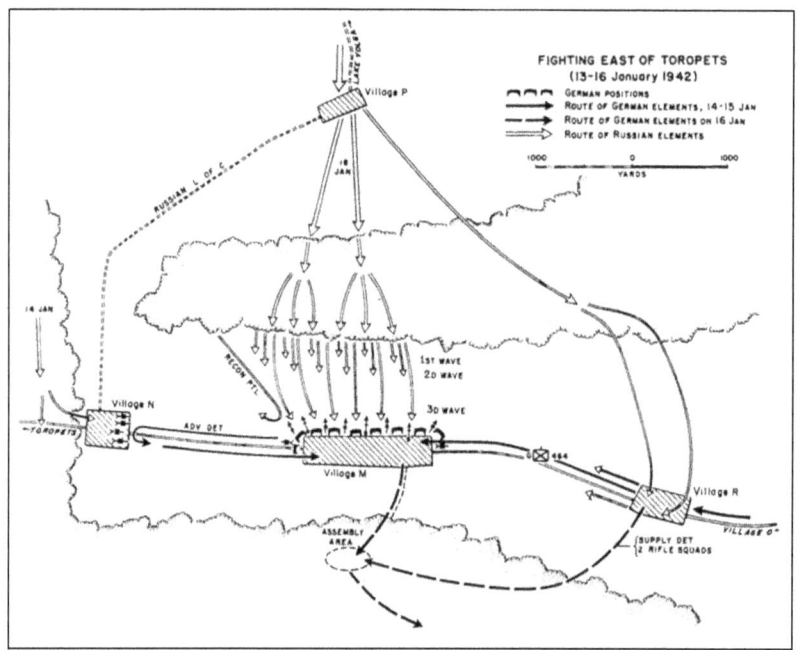

FIGHTING EAST OF TOROPETS (13-16 January 1942)

trucks, reached Village O, 5 miles east of Village M. Upon its arrival at Village O, a supply unit, which was fleeing eastward toward Rzhev before the powerful Russian offensive, indicated that strong contingents of Russian troops from the north had cut the German supply route in the forest west of Village N. Using civilian labor, the Russians had constructed a road at least 30 miles long that led south through the large forest bypassing Toropets to the east. The company commander, Lieutenant Viehmann, decided to establish local security in Village O, spend the night there, and continue westward on foot the next morning in order to see what was going on. During the night a few Russian civilians slipped out of the village, established contact with the Russian troops, and supplied them with intelligence regarding the German dispositions.

At dawn on 15 January, after posting security details, the company started out and arrived in Village M without having made contact with the Russian's. As the company's advance element approached Village N, the Germans noticed a large group of soldiers in German uniform standing in the road, beckoning to them. That these soldiers were not Germans became evident when the antitank gun moving up behind the advance element was suddenly fired upon. The company's other antitank guns covered the advance element's withdrawal to Village M, where it rejoined the main body of the company. The prime mover of the lead gun was lost during this action. The Russians, however, did not follow up their attack.

In Village M the company set up hasty defenses against an attack from the north and west and tried to determine the strength and intentions of the opposing Russian force. From a vantage point in Village M it was possible to observe the eastern edge of Village N, where the Russians were building snow positions and moving four antitank guns into position. There was an exchange of fire but no indication of an impending Russian attack. During the hours of darkness Company G built snow positions along the western and northern edges of Village M, while the aforementioned supply unit occupied Village R, about one mile east of Village M, and took measures to secure it, particularly from the north.

During the night of 15-16 January reconnaissance patrols reported that the Russians were continuing their defensive preparations in Village N and that their line of communications was the road leading north from there.

On 16 January between 0400 and 0500 a 50-man Russian reconnaissance patrol approached the northwest corner of Village M on skis. Although the Russian patrol had been detected, it was allowed to come very close before it was taken under fire. Approximately 10 men of the patrol escaped and three were taken prisoner; the rest were killed before they could reach the German position.

According to the statements of the three prisoners, two Russian divisions were moving south toward Village M. On 16

January Villages M and R were to be captured. What the prisoners either did not know or refused to tell, was that the Russians, attacking in force across frozen Lake Volga, had broken through the German positions west of the 253d Infantry Division 2 days before and had pushed on to the south. Thus, Viehmann was unaware of the true German situation.

Since the Russians in Village N remained passive, Viehmann decided to concentrate on defending his village against an attack from the north. The deep snow caused some difficulties; for instance, machineguns had to be mounted on antiaircraft tripods so that a satisfactory field of fire could be obtained.

About 0800 on 16 January the company's observation post identified three Russian columns moving south toward the forest north of Village M. Except for antitank guns these columns did not seem to be equipped with heavy weapons. Around 1000 the first Russians appeared at the southern edge of the forest, some 1,000 yards from the German defensive positions. At 1020 the Russian center and right-wing columns attacked with antitank guns and infantry. Just a short time before this attack Company G had dispatched two rifle squads to Village R to reinforce the supply unit there, since the Russian left-wing column was headed in that direction.

The first wave of Russian infantry, some 400 men strong, emerged from the forest on a broad front. It was evident that the 3-foot snow was causing them great difficulty. The concentrated fire of the German heavy weapons succeeded in halting the attack after it had advanced about 200 yards.

After a short while a second, equally large wave emerged from the forest. It advanced in the tracks of the first and carried the attack forward, over and beyond the line of dead. The Russian antitank fire became heavier, being directed against the German machinegun positions, which the Russians had spotted. As a result, several machineguns were destroyed; some changed their positions frequently in an effort to dodge the Russian fire.

The Russians advanced an additional 200 yards, then bogged down under the effective German small arms fire. They sustained heavy losses which, however, were compensated for by the reinforcements pouring down south into the forest from Village P. Viehmann estimated that the Russians committed the equivalent of two regiments in this action.

By 1100 the Russian left-wing column had reached a point 150 yards from the German positions in Village R, where the terrain was more favorable for the attacker than that north of Village M. The supply unit and the two rifle squads defending Village R could no longer be reinforced because the road from Village M was under constant Russian fire.

Realizing that his position would become untenable within the next few hours, Viehmann ordered his men to prepare to evacuate Village M. A few men with minor wounds were detailed to trample a path through the deep snow from Village M toward the forest to the south in order to facilitate a quick withdrawal. The troops in Village R were also to withdraw to the same forest if pressed too heavily by the Russians.

The members of the third Russian assault wave emerged from the forest unarmed. However, they armed themselves quickly with the weapons of their fallen comrades and continued the attack. Meanwhile, Village R was taken and the Russians closed in on Village M from the east. The Germans were now very low on ammunition, having expended almost 20,000 rounds during the fighting.

About 1300 Company G, after destroying its mortars and antitank guns, evacuated Village M. Viehmann planned to make contact with the German troops in Village O by withdrawing through the forest south of Village M. He ordered the evacuation of the wounded, then withdrew with the main body of the company, and left behind a light machinegun and an antitank gun to provide covering fire and to simulate the presence of a larger force. After the gun crews had expended all the ammunition, they destroyed the breech operating mechanism of the antitank gun and withdrew toward the forest. About halfway there they were fired on by the Russians who had meanwhile entered Village M. The retreating Germans managed to escape without losses because the Russians did not pursue them into the forest.

During the next 3 days the company marched—with almost no halts for rest—through the deep snow that blanketed the dense forest, relying heavily on a compass in the absence of familiar landmarks. On 19 January, after bypassing Village O, which was found to be occupied by the Russians, it finally reestablished contact with the 253d Infantry Division. Only then did the company learn that all forces on the German front south of and parallel to Lake Volga had been withdrawn in the meantime.

In this action deep snow hampered the movements of both the attacking Russians and the defending Germans. Only by trampling a path in the snow before its withdrawal from Village M, did Company G avoid being trapped by the Russians.

The appearance of a Russian reconnaissance patrol in German uniform was a frequent occurrence; however, the number of disguised

Russians encountered on 15 January in Village N was unusually large. As so often happened during the winter of 1941-42, the Russians attacked in several waves on a given front, each successive wave passing over the dead of the preceding and carrying the attack forward to a point where it, too, was destroyed. Some waves started out unarmed and recovered the weapons from their fallen comrades.

Russian Infantry Attacks a German-Held Town (January 1942)

While the German troops west of Moscow tried to weather the Russian winter offensive and maintain their precarious lines of communication in the Rzhev-Velikiye Luki area, Marshal Timoshenko's forces launched a strong attack against Army Group South. In mid-January 1942 they attacked the German positions along the Donets River between Kharkov and Slavyansk and achieved a deep penetration near Izyum. The Russians smashed through the weakly held German positions and advanced westward, attempting simultaneously to widen the gap by attacking southward. In that direction the Russian objectives were Slavyansk and the industrial Donets Basin, whose capture would lead to the collapse of the German front in southern Russia.

The German troops along the Donets River had not expected Russian winter offensive since the opposing forces were believed to be weak and incapable of launching one. Because of the shortage of winter equipment, the Germans had been forced to leave only outposts along the Donets River and in isolated villages, while their main forces occupied winter quarters far to the rear. In most instances the defending units were unable to delay the progress of the Russian offensive because the attacking troops simply bypassed them.

Toward the end of January the temperature dropped to -50° F. The snow was about 3 feet deep. The weather was clear and a biting east wind prevailed.

There was light Russian air activity, with fighters and light bombers intervening occasionally in the ground fighting. The Luftwaffe rarely made an appearance.

Timoshenko's forces were at full combat strength, well armed, appropriately equipped for winter combat, and fed adequate rations. By contrast, the German units were at 65 percent of T/O strength and short of winter clothing and equipment, but their rations were plentiful.

By defending the town of Khristishehe against attacks from the north, northeast, and east, the 1st Battalion of the German 196th Infantry Regiment was to block any further Russian

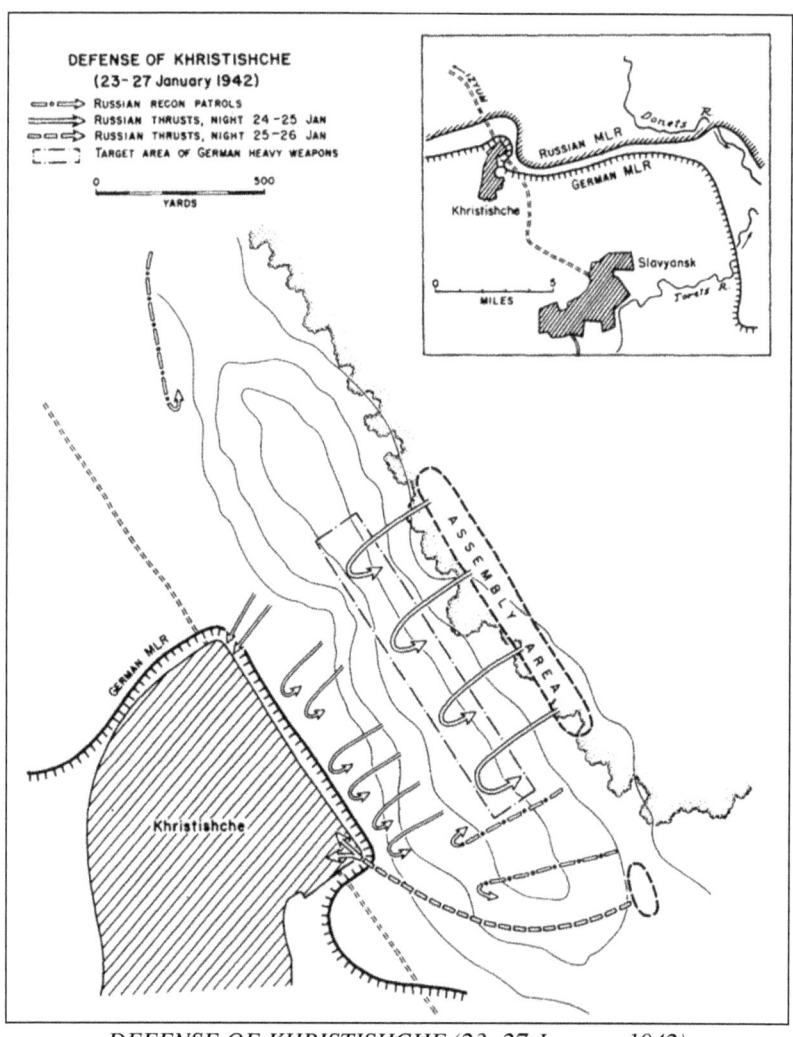

DEFENSE OF KHRISTISHCHE (23- 27 January 1942)

advance along the road to Slavyansk (map above). To the south, reconnaissance patrols were to maintain contact with a few strong points located in nearby villages. To the west the battalion was to keep in close contact with the adjacent unit of its regiment. Snow positions had been established at the edges of Khristishehe because it was impossible to dig in the frozen soil. The battalion's field of fire extended up to 2,200 yards north and south. To the east lay a long ridge, beyond which there was a large forest held by strong Russian forces.

During the night of 23-24 January a Siberian rifle regiment with twenty-four 76.5-mm. guns, advancing westward, reached a point 1 mile northeast of Khristishche. It fired on a German reconnaissance patrol, which withdrew southwestward leaving behind one wounded man, who disclosed to the Russians that there were two German regiments in and around Khristishche.

On the morning of 24 January a Russian reconnaissance patrol in platoon strength attempted to approach Khristishche, but was almost completely wiped out by German machinegun fire and snipers. Russian reconnaissance patrols looking down from the hill observed lively movement in the town, but made no attempt to advance any farther during daytime.

According to information obtained from a subsequently captured Russian officer, the Siberian rifle regiment received the following order on 24 January:

The Germans have been beaten along the entire front. They still cling to isolated villages to retard the victorious Russian advance.

Khristishche is being defended by severely mauled German units, whose morale is low. They must be destroyed so that the Russian advance to Slavyansk can continue.

At 2115 on 24 January two battalions of the regiment will attack Khristishche without artillery preparation and will advance to the western edge of the town. The 3d Battalion will follow behind the 1st and 2d Battalions and clear the village of all Germans. Then the 3d Battalion will occupy the northeastern edge of Khristishche on both sides of the road leading to Izyum, facing southeast. Reconnaissance patrols will probe in the direction of Slavyansk. One ski company* will reinforce each assault battalion. The ski units will enter Khristishche without permitting anything to divert them from this objective. During the day preceding the attack the battalion and regimental artillery and mortars will fire for adjustment on all important targets. However, the Germans must not be led to expect our attack.

Throughout 24 January the positions of the 1st Battalion of the German 196th Infantry Regiment were hit by intermittent fire from light artillery and heavy mortars. Apparently this fire was directed by Russian observers on the ridge northeast of Khristishche.

At dusk the Germans increased their vigilance. In the snow trenches the sentries, dressed in white parkas, were doubled and posted at intervals of approximately thirty feet. Observation was made very difficult by the east wind, which blew snow into the men's faces. The sentries were relieved every 30 minutes.

At 2115 the sentries of Company C observed rapidly approaching figures near the boundary between their sector and that of Company B. They tried to open fire with their machineguns but found them frozen. Finally, one sentry was able to give the alarm by firing his carbine. By this time Russian assault troops on skis had been observed along the entire battalion front firing carbines and signal pistols and throwing hand grenades. The only German machinegun which would fire was the one that had been kept indoors.

The Russian surprise raid did not proceed as planned because the attackers were unable to jump over the 4-foot snow wall on skis and because most of them were not immediately ready to fire since they carried their weapons slung across their backs. The Russians were therefore repulsed, except for those who penetrated into the extreme north end of the town. Twenty-five Russians occupied the first house but were wiped out within 5 minutes by hand grenades.

Meanwhile, the German mortars and infantry howitzers laid down a barrage on the ridge northeast of the town. Two Russian battalions, which had just gained the ridge, were caught in the barrage and turned back.

The 1st Battalion took 43 prisoners, including some wounded. Over a hundred Russians lay dead in and around the German positions. The Germans had lost 2 dead, 8 wounded, and 3 suffering from frostbite.

Throughout the night the Germans heard loud cries and shouting from the forest, followed by submachinegun and rifle fire. Russian prisoners subsequently stated that the commissars assigned to the platoons and companies were trying to reorganize their units. They were unsuccessful in this attempt until the following morning (25 January), by which time several Russian soldiers had been shot and the regimental commander replaced.

That same morning a Russian combat patrol of GO men approached Khristishche from the north but was wiped out some 500 yards from the German positions. In the afternoon two Russian reconnaissance patrols of 30 men each, supported by 3 machine gunners and 20 snipers, advanced toward the town from the southeast in single file. They were stopped halfway to their objective by German small arms fire. Approximately 20 men ran back over the hill, only to be stopped by their commissars and shot for cowardice. The intervening hours before darkness passed without incident.

The Russian troops built snow positions at the edge of the forest, set up observation posts and combat outposts on the crest of the hill, and dug emplacements for their artillery and mortars. Each squad built a shelter hut with tree trunks and branches, on top of which snow was packed. These shelters were built close together in an irregular pattern. The infantry howitzers and heavy mortars received five extra issues of ammunition, which were stored in nearby shelters.

That night a Russian combat patrol of 50 men under the command of an officer approached Khristishche from the east. The patrol was armed with 8 submachineguns, 2 pistols, 2 signal pistols, 38 automatic rifles, 2 light machineguns, each with 500 rounds of tracer ammunition, and 8 hand grenades per man. Most of the men wore padded winter uniforms and felt boots with leather soles; those, however, who could speak German were dressed in German uniforms. The patrol was to occupy the first houses and then send a message to the rear, where a reinforced company was kept in readiness to follow up the patrol's attack and to occupy Khristishche.

About 0130, while an icy east wind was blowing, five figures approached the two German sentries near the eastern corner of the town and called out from a distance, "Hello, 477th Regiment! Hello, comrades!" The Germans, who because of the whirling snow could see only about 60 feet ahead, challenged them from a distance of 30 feet with "Halt! Password!" The answer was "Don't fire! We are German comrades!" They continued to advance. The sentries now noticed a number of men about 50 feet behind the 5 soldiers who were approaching. Again they called "Password, or we fire!" Again the answer was "Don't shoot! We are German comrades!" Meanwhile the 5 Russians in German uniforms had approached to within 20 feet, whereupon they hurled hand grenades, which wounded 1 German sentry. The other fired his carbine to give the alarm, but in doing so was shot by the Russians, who immediately headed for the first house, followed by the main body of the combat patrol.

The Russians tossed hand grenades into the first house just as the men of the German squad which occupied the building ran out the back door without suffering any casualties. Throwing hand grenades and firing carbines and machineguns from the hip, the German infantrymen tried to stop the Russians who closed in from three sides. The German squad was pushed back to the second house, and the Russians immediately occupied the first one, set up two machineguns, and opened fire on M Company men, who were coming up on the double.

The Russians threw hand grenades and explosives through a window into the second house in order to wipe out the German squad occupying this house. At first this attempt was unsuccessful, but when the house caught fire that German squad was forced to evacuate. It got outside through a damaged wall on the far side of the house. By this time the commander of

Company M had taken charge of the situation and had launched a counterthrust with company headquarters personnel, reserve squads, and the squad that had initially occupied the first house. Throwing hand grenades and firing their weapons on the run, the counterattacking Germans drove the Russians from Khristishche within a few minutes. Eight Russian enlisted men and one commissar manned two machineguns in the first house, where they resisted to the last man.

Upon noticing the signal equipment that the Russians had left behind in the first house, the German company commander correctly concluded that a Russian main force was assembled outside the village, waiting for the signal to advance. He called for artillery support against the suspected Russian jumpoff positions. The artillery fire began a minute later and probably prevented the Russian company from following up the attack. The remainder of the night passed quietly.

On the morning of 26 January the sun shone brightly, and the east wind continued to blow across Khristishche. Quiet reigned until 1000, when the Russian artillery started to shell the northeastern part of the town. Harassing fire continued until 1500.

At 1100, as the battalion commander was making his rounds of the German positions, a sentry from Company C reported that he had observed some suspicious movements on the forward slope of the hill east of Khristishche. A few Russian corpses which had been lying there had already vanished that morning, and he believed that the small piles of snow some 200 yards east of his post had increased in size.

The battalion commander observed the forward slope of the hill with binoculars for 1 hour, although a cold wind was blowing. He discovered a number of Russians hiding in the deep snow and cautiously piling up snow in front of them to increase their cover. The German sentries fired their carbines at every suspicious-looking pile of snow; no further movements were observed.

Russian prisoners subsequently stated that 1 Russian platoon of 40 men had been ordered to approach the town under cover of darkness and to dig into the snow. After daybreak this platoon was to push further toward the town in order to launch a surprise attack against it at nightfall. The platoon maintained wire communication with the rear.

Despite the bitter cold, the Russians remained in the snow for about 10 hours without being able to raise their heads or shift their bodies. Yet not one of them suffered frostbite.

On the basis of previous experience, the Russian commander ordered a mass attack without artillery support for that night (26-27 January). The fact that there were snow flurries and a strong east wind, may have induced him to make this decision.

The Russians assembled 3 battalions, totaling 1,500 men, for the attack. Two battalions were echeloned in the first assault wave, while the third battalion followed about 350 yards behind. The Russian regimental command post remained at the edge of the forest. Each company had 20 submachineguns, 35 automatic rifles, 10 rifles with telescopic sights, 8 heavy machineguns (drum fed), 5 light mortars, 12 pistols, and 2 signal pistols, as well as a number of rifles with fixed bayonets. Each man was issued three hand grenades and an ample supply of ammunition. All men wore padded winter clothing and felt boots.

At 0330 the Russian regiment started its attack. Any noise that the approaching Russians might have made was drowned out by the howling wind. The battalions advanced in close formation without leaving any intervals between units. The companies marched abreast in columns of three's and four's, with an interval of 5 to 10 paces between them. Without commands the Russians marched in close order to within 50 yards of the German positions and then began their assault amid wild shouting.

Only a few Russians broke into the German position; they

were greeted with such a devastating hail of fire from the alert defenders that the dense Russian columns were mowed down, row after row. Nevertheless, those who survived attacked again and again.

Then the German artillery fire hit the Russian reserve battalion, which was completely dispersed. After half an hour the impetus of the attack had spent itself. Within two or three yards of the German positions the enemy dead or wounded had piled up to a height of several feet. The Russians suffered about 900 casualties in the engagement.

Khristishche remained in German hands because the garrison was alert and had learned to take proper care of its weapons.

Company G Struggles Against Overwhelming Odds (March 1942)

The following action shows a Russian regiment attacking eastward in an attempt to cut off some German units and link up with friendly forces moving in from the opposite direction. The attack methods employed by the Russian infantry showed that the troops were inadequately trained. The infantry units emerged from their jumpoff position in a disorderly manner, having the appearance of a disorganized herd that suddenly emerged from a forest. As soon as the Germans opened fire, panic developed in the ranks of the attack force. The infantrymen had to be driven forward by three or four officers with drawn pistols. In many instances any attempt to retreat or even to glance backward was punished with immediate execution. There was virtually no mutual fire support or coordinated fire.

Typical of Russian infantry tactics was the tenacity with which the attack was repeated over and over again. The Russians never abandoned ground which they had gained in an attack. Frequently, isolated Russian soldiers would feign death, only to surprise approaching Germans by suddenly coming to life and firing at them from close range.

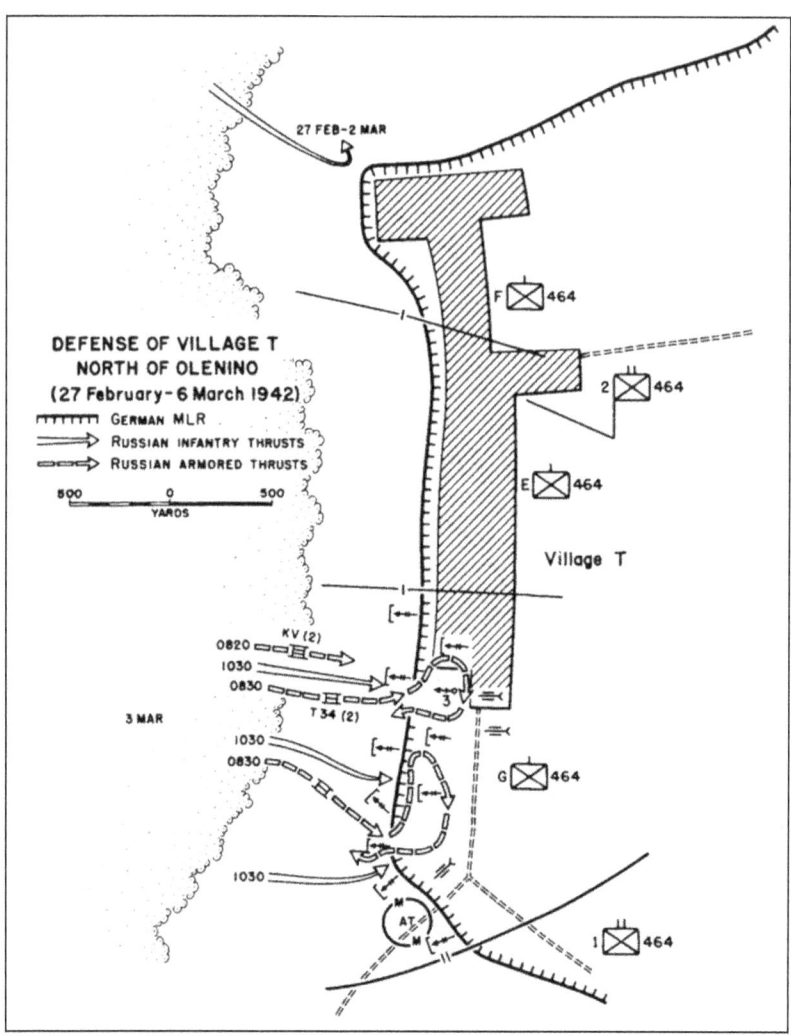

DEFENSE OF VILLAGE T NORTH OF OLENINO

In February 1942 the 2d Battalion of the 464th German Infantry Regiment occupied snow positions without bunkers or dugouts along the western edge of Village T, situated north of Olenino near the rail line leading from Rzhev to Velikiye Luki (see map above). German reconnaissance patrols probing through the forest west of that village had been unable to establish contact with the Russians. Toward the end of February a reconnaissance patrol ascertained the presence of Russian forces in the forest. Subsequent information obtained from local inhabitants indicated that the Russians were being reinforced for an attack.

From 27 February to 2 March, detachments, consisting of about 80 Russians each, attacked daily in the same sector and at the same time. The attacks took place about 1 hour after sunrise and were directed against a point at the northwest edge of Village T. Every one of them was unsuccessful, the attacking Russians being wiped out before they could reach the German position.

On the evening of 2 March a Russian deserter reported that his infantry regiment, supported by six tanks, would attack Company G's sector, which was south of the village. To strengthen the defense of his sector the company commander, Lieutenant Viehmann, placed three 37-mm. antitank guns behind the MLR and planted antitank mines across the road leading southwestward. Although his unit was under-strength, Viehmann ordered each platoon to form a reserve detachment of 10 men for a possible counterthrust.

At daybreak on 3 March two Russian heavy tanks of the KV type, painted white to blend with the landscape, were spotted standing at the edge of the forest about 500 yards in front of Company G's sector. At 0820 Russian aircraft bombed the village, while the two tanks, about 150 yards apart, advanced another 100 yards, stopped, and opened fire at the most conspicuous German fortifications. At 0830 four more Russian tanks, this time T34's, emerged from the forest. They paired off, penetrated the right and center of Company G's MLR, and rolled up the stretch between the two points of penetration. Encountering no effective resistance, they pushed deeper into the German defensive position while providing mutual fire support. The three German 37-mm. antitank guns proved ineffective against the T34's and were quickly knocked out, as were a number of German heavy weapons. However, without immediate infantry support the Russian tanks were incapable of achieving any further results.

It was not until 2 hours later that approximately 300 Russian riflemen attacked from the forest, while the two KV tanks stood still and the T34's roamed at will through the depth of the German defensive position. Hampered by the deep snow, the infantry had to bunch up and advance along the tank tracks, offering easy targets during their slow movement. Despite the loss of many of their heavy weapons, the German defenders mustered sufficient strength to repel the Russian attack and to force the infantry to withdraw into the forest, the tanks following soon afterward.

A short time later the four T34's reappeared. This time each tank carried a rifle squad. Additional infantry supported the attack. When the T34's re-entered the German MLR three of them were eliminated by German infantrymen who threw antitank mines into their paths. The Russian foot infantry elements advanced 350 yards from the forest's edge before being pinned down by German mortar fire. The one tank that remained intact quickly withdrew into the forest, followed by the Russian infantry. Throughout the day the two KV's remained in the German outpost area and fired on everything that moved within the German position.

Russian prisoners taken during the fighting stated that the riflemen mounted on tanks had been ordered to establish themselves within the German defensive position to support the Russian infantry's attack. These statements were confirmed when it was discovered that a number of small Russian detachments had infiltrated the German outpost area, from where they refused to be dislodged despite the severe cold. After dark, German combat patrols were finally able to move out and liquidate them.

All was quiet on 4 March. The next day the Russians resumed the attack all along the 2d Battalion sector with a force estimated at 2 to 3 infantry regiments and supported by 16 tanks. While the Russian artillery confined itself to harassing the German rear area, the mortars laid down intensive fire, whose effect was insignificant because of the deep snow. Severe fighting continued unabated until evening. After dark the Russians broke into the southern part of Village T at several points. By that time severe losses in men and materiel had greatly weakened the defending force. Nevertheless, the Germans held the northern part of Village T until the morning of 6 March, when they withdrew to a new position 2 miles farther east.

In this engagement the Russians demonstrated extraordinary skill in approaching through the snow-covered forests without attracting the attention of the Germans. They permitted small German reconnaissance patrols to pass at will to create the impression that the forest was clear.

The four limited attacks that preceded the main assault were either feints or reconnaissance thrusts in force. By repeating them against the same sector on 4 subsequent days, the Russians probably intended to divert German defense forces to that point.

During the main assault the teamwork between Russian tanks and infantry was inadequate. In this particular engagement the Russian infantry showed little aggressiveness, and the tanks had to advance alone to break up the German defense system before the infantry jumped off. Actually, the long interval between tank and infantry attacks had precisely the opposite effect. It is true that the Russian tank attack threw the German defense into temporary confusion, because the 37-mm. antitank guns were ineffective against the T34's and KV's and the German infantry lacked experience in combatting tanks at close range. Moreover, the two KV tanks acted as armored assault guns and prevented all movements within the German position. These often-used tactics were successful as long as the Germans did not have antitank guns whose projectiles could pierce the armor of these tanks. However, by the time the Russian infantry launched its attack two hours later, the defenders were able to overcome their initial fear of the giant KV tanks and to rally sufficient strength to frustrate the Russian infantry attack. When the Russian armor attacked for the second time, the German infantry knew how to cope with it effectively.

As in many other instances, the lower echelon Russian commanders revealed a certain lack of initiative in the execution of orders. Individual units were simply given a mission or a time schedule to which they adhered rigidly. This operating procedure had its obvious weaknesses. While the Russian soldier had the innate faculty of adapting himself easily to technological innovations and overcoming mechanical difficulties, the lower echelon commanders seemed incapable of coping with sudden changes in the situation and acting on their own initiative. Fear of punishment in the event of failure may have motivated their reluctance to make independent decisions.

The Russian troops employed in this action seemed to be particularly immune to extreme cold. Individual snipers hid in the deep snow throughout day or night, even at temperatures as low as -50°F. In temperatures of -40° F. and below, the German machineguns often failed to function, and below -60° F. some of the rifles failed to fire. In these temperatures the oil or grease congealed, jamming the bolt mechanism. Locally procured sunflower oil was used as a lubricant when available, as it guaranteed the proper functioning of weapons in subzero temperatures.

Company G Annihilates a Russian Elite Unit (March 1942)

During March 1942 Russian pressure from the north and west forced the Germans to make a limited withdrawal northwest of Rzhev. In late March the 2d Battalion of the German 464th Infantry Regiment, including Company G, established defensive positions in Village S, about 12 miles northwest of Olenino. The village was situated on level ground and was faced by forests to the north, east, and south (map opposite). The terrain to the west

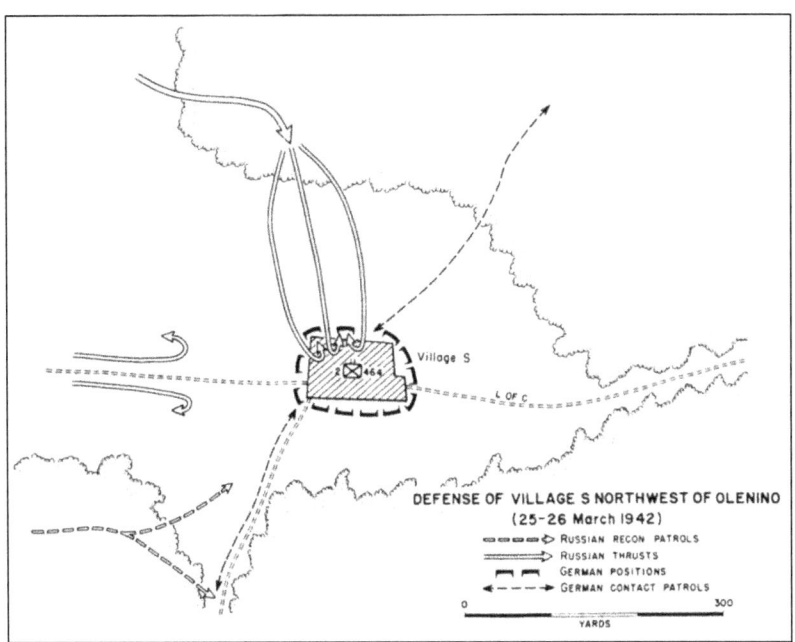

DEFENSE OF VILLAGE S NORTHWEST OF OLENINO
(25-26 March 1942)

was open, permitting the defenders to detect at an early moment the approach of any Russian forces coming from that direction. Since the German forces in the area were not strong enough to establish a continuous defense line, the village was organized for perimeter defense. The battalion constructed snow positions above the ground, excavation of the frozen soil being impossible, and maintained contact with adjacent units by sending patrols through the forests around the village. On 25 March the low temperature was -44° F. and 3 feet of snow covered the ground. On that day the 2d Battalion repelled several attacks from the west, inflicting heavy losses on the Russians, who then intensified their patrol activity.

Before dawn on 26 March a reconnaissance patrol sent out by Company G returned from the forest bordering Village S to the north without having encountered enemy troops. The distance from the edge of the forest to the defense perimeter measured approximately 150 yards. Half an hour after the return of the German patrol 100 Russians suddenly emerged from the forest and attacked Company G at the northwestern part of the defense ring. The Russians participating in the attack were armed with submachineguns and moved on skis, which made the small force exceedingly mobile in the snow-covered terrain. In addition, every third man carried a frangible grenade in his pocket, presumably for the purpose of setting fire to the village. Several Russians literally blew up when their frangible grenades were struck by bullets and exploded. Because of the severe cold some of the German machineguns failed to function, and the Russians succeeded in penetrating the German positions.

Half an hour later Company G counterattacked in order to eliminate the penetration. The Russians fought tenaciously, and there was violent hand-to-hand combat. By 1200 Company G had recaptured the positions. Eighty-nine Russians were killed and nine, including two seriously wounded, taken prisoner. All of the attackers were NCO candidates who had been promised battlefield promotions if they captured Village S.

While Company G was mopping up the area, brief hand-to-hand fighting suddenly flared up at two points where prostrate Russians, suddenly coming to life, jumped to their feet and assaulted the German soldiers.

This example illustrates how effectively the Russian riflemen exploited the terrain when approaching the enemy, even in deep snow and extreme cold. The attack was conducted skillfully and silently, and fullest use was made of the element of surprise. The entire assault force rushed out of the forest and attacked in a single wave. However, when the surprise attack did not result in the immediate capture of the village but led to a struggle for the German positions, the operation lost its tactical value since the Russian unit had gone into battle without any support. Instead of breaking off the engagement and withdrawing, the Russians continued fighting until their entire force was wiped out.

This action, however, does not lend itself to generalization since a special Russian unit composed of noncommissioned officer candidates was involved. Except for the resistance offered to the German advance in the summer of 1941 by certain Russian elite formations, no other Russian units had fought so violently and tenaciously.

During World War II the training status of different Russian units showed such great variations that generalizations based on the performance of individual units are not permissible. As in any other army, there were both good and indifferent units among the innumerable divisions which opposed the Germans. Training courses at Russian service schools were conducted with great thoroughness, and even senior officers were subjected to the rigors of the ordinary training schedule. Training was not limited to the achievement of military proficiency; it was constantly overshadowed by political indoctrination designed to imbue every soldier with the ideological principles involved in the life-and-death struggle.

Company G Recaptures Hill 726 (October 1942)

During the spring and summer of 1942 the Germans strengthened the Rzhev salient and eliminated Russian forces that had gained a foothold west of the Vyazma-Rzhev rail line. The salient gradually became one of the strongest defense lines the Germans had built in Russia. In the early autumn Marshal Zhukov launched an offensive against the Rzhev salient to divert German forces from the Stalingrad front and to eliminate this potential threat to the Russian capital. In this action, which is the last one in the series concerning the fighting west of Moscow, Company G resisted the onslaught of fresh Russian troops who had recently arrived from training centers in Siberia.

In mid-September Russian infantry supported by tanks seized Hill 726, some 10 miles north of Olenino. Once the Russians had wrested it from the Germans, they withdrew their tanks and left an infantry company of about 75 men to defend the newly

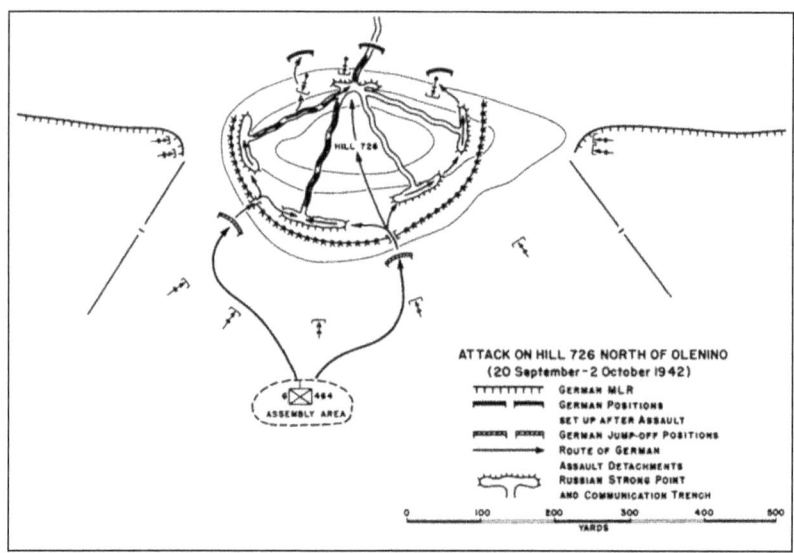

ATTACK ON HILL 726 NORTH OF OLENINO
(20 September-2 October 1942)

won position. This hill now constituted a dent in the German MLR and afforded a sweeping view of the German rear area, thus hampering movements. Its rapid recapture was of vital importance to the Germans (map above).

The Russian defense system on the hill was not organized in a continuous line, but rather in the form of strong points. The positions were quite deep, afforded overhead cover, and were so well camouflaged that they could be detected only at very close range. The communication trenches leading to the rear were deep enough only for crawling. All machineguns were emplaced so as to deliver only frontal fire. Mortars were emplaced on the reverse slope of the hill, and large quantities of ammunition and hand grenades had been stored in the strong points. A belt of wooden mines—to which German detectors did not respond—extended almost completely around the hill. Gaps had been left in the mine belt to permit passage of friendly patrols. Before the attack German reconnaissance patrols were able to identify these lanes.

Company G made five or six attempts to retake Hill 726, but

failed; in each case the attack was halted at the very beginning because of heavy casualties incurred from mines and massed mortar fire. The Russians defended the hill with extreme tenacity. The company commander, Captain Viehmann, observed that the Russians confined their activity to the hours of darkness. During the day their positions appeared deserted. Russian reconnaissance patrols were very active, but only between midnight and dawn.

Viehmann decided to launch a surprise attack at dusk on 2 October. He selected 30 men who, together with two flame thrower teams, were to make up the assault detachments. Six machineguns were to follow directly behind. After seizure of the hill, an intrenching team was to move in with previously prepared barbed wire obstacles, set them up on the reverse side of the hill, and establish defensive positions. All men in the assault detachments were equipped with sub-machineguns and issued an ample supply of hand grenades. They were familiar with the terrain, including Hill 726 itself and the Russian MLR.

Under cover of darkness and unnoticed by the Russians, the assault troops moved from their assembly area into the jumpoff positions. At the scheduled time the two companies along the flanks of the German MLR facing the right and left sides of the hill as well as the machine-guns located on the southern slope poured fire into the Russian positions. While the German troops in the MLR diverted the enemy's attention by sudden shouting, the assault elements attacked and penetrated the Russian mine belt through two previously identified gaps.

The defending Russians were taken completely by surprise. The fire and shouting coming from all sides confused them as to the true direction of the attack. They were further thrown off balance by the German flame throwers, despite the fact that the latter failed to function after only a few bursts.

Nevertheless, the Russians did not give way to panic or abandon their positions, but struggled to the bitter end. After about an hour of hand-to-hand fighting the entire hill was in German hands, as were 20 Russian prisoners. The initial German objective, to cut Russian communications to the rear, had been achieved early in the attack. The Russian MLR was thereby out of contact with the defenders on the hill, who apparently were not alert enough to summon assistance from the rear before being cut off.

Once the hill was taken, the Germans immediately dispatched two listening sentries to points about 30 yards in the front of their lines, set up barbed wire obstacles, and otherwise prepared their defensive positions. Within 2 hours a continuous line of wire entanglements stretched across the crest of the hill.

About an hour after the completion of these defenses one of the sentries reported the approach of about 40 Russians. All intrenching work was immediately suspended and the defense positions were quickly manned. Soon thereafter the second sentry confirmed the report of the first. The gap in the wire obstacle line which had until then been left open for the men stationed at the listening post was closed.

At a given signal the Germans opened fire just as the screaming Russians began their counterattack. Rushing headlong into the wire entanglements, which they had failed to spot in advance, the Russians were cut down by German defensive fire concentrated on that zone. Only three of the attackers were able to regain the safety of their jumpoff position.

The next day the Russians directed heavy harassing fire against Hill 726, but made no further attempts to conduct a concerted infantry attack.

THE STRUGGLE FOR SHELTER (DECEMBER 1941)

By General-Major Burkhart Mueiler-Hillebrand, General-Major Heilmuth Reinhardt, and others

The winter of 1941-42 was particularly severe and the fighting on many sectors of the front centered around inhabited localities that could offer shelter from the cold. In mid-December a German patrol captured an operations order that revealed that the Russians planned to attack southwestward along a road leading from the direction of Lisichansk, on the Donets, with the intention of disrupting the German lines of communication. On 18 December the 203d Infantry Regiment moved into a new battle position in and around Berestovaya, a village situated along the expected Russian axis of advance. The regiment organized its center of resistance around the stone buildings in the center of the village (map below).

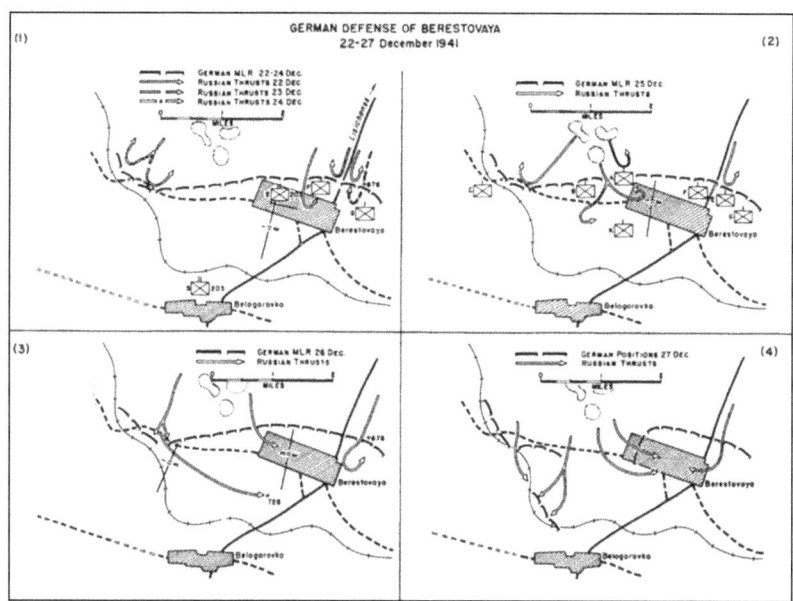

GERMAN DEFENSE OF BERESTOVAYA 22-27 December 1941

The 203d had been engaged in heavy defensive fighting for several weeks, and its combat efficiency had dropped sharply. The average strength of the infantry companies had been reduced to approximately 50 riflemen, and the regiment had lost about one-third of its heavy weapons.

Sprawling villages and a few trees were predominant features of the rolling landscape around Berestovaya, whose stone houses— rare in this part of Russia—provided ample shelter against December temperatures, which averaged about 15° F. The snow cover varied from 4 inches to several feet in depth.

From 18 through 22 December the Russians deployed their forces and pushed back one German outpost after another, an indication that a major attack was imminent. On the evening of 22 December the 2d Battalion was hit by a Russian infantry force of regimental strength. German defensive fire succeeded in stopping the Russian advance on both sides of the Lisichansk-Belogorovka road; however, a German strong point on F Company's left flank was overrun and Russian elements penetrated Berestovaya as far as the 2d Battalion command post. The battalion commander then committed his reserves and restored the situation.

On 23 December the Russians made unsuccessful piecemeal attacks in company to battalion strength against the 2d Battalion sector astride the Lisichansk-Belogorovka road. After darkness had fallen, the Russians fired a brief artillery concentration against the forward positions of G company in the area east of the road; then they attacked the company with 2 battalions of infantry supported by 10 tanks and broke through near Hill 676. German artillery was then brought to bear on the Russian armor, forcing it to withdraw, and the infantry, deprived of tank support, was unable to advance. The Germans thereupon committed Companies I and K of the reserve battalion and sealed off the Russian penetration.

On the 24th the Russians, using only infantry, attacked along the road and, for the first time, against the left flank of the adjacent 1st Battalion.

On Christmas morning the Russians attacked along the road and eastward with two battalions of infantry, but were stopped by artillery fire. Shortly afterward, two Russian assault groups, each consisting of one to two companies supported by mortar fire, debouched from draws northwest of Berestovaya and attacked A and C Companies. Despite their numerical inferiority, the Germans managed to repulse these attacks.

About 1400, in the face of a sharp east wind, 12 Russian tanks suddenly emerged from the same draws and made a surprise attack toward Berestovaya from the west. Accompanied by infantry, the tanks advanced slowly and brought the German strong points under fire. Within an hour the tanks had broken through Company A's position, where 40 men were trying to hold a 1,000-yard-wide sector. A few of the tanks broke off from their accompanying infantry and moved southward toward the railroad embankment, but withdrew after two tanks had been lost to antitank fire.

Company K counterattacked from the south and cleared the village of those elements that had broken through its defenses. Headquarters Company of the 3d Battalion and I Company were moved up from Belogorovka and committed; by 2100 the German MLR was restored.

The heavy casualties that had been suffered in the action up to that point forced the 203d Infantry Regiment to reorganize the three battalions being assigned adjoining sectors, with the 3d Battalion in the center, flanked by the 1st and 2d on the left and right, respectively. Each battalion held one company in reserve.

At dawn on the 26th the Russians began heavy attacks in the area between Berestovaya and that portion of the rail line due west of the village. Seventeen Russian tanks, accompanied by infantry, moved against the right wing of the 1st Battalion, smashing B Company's position. As the Russians reached the railroad embankment they were halted by German artillery fire. Some of the Russian tanks moved on southeastward toward Hill 728, a conspicuous plateau in the otherwise rolling terrain. The hill offered no cover to the Germans who could not hold it against the Russian tank fire and therefore withdrew southward to the railroad. In order to strengthen the regiment's defenses, division moved one infantry battalion and a squadron of dismounted bicycle infantry to Belogorovka.

German ground-support aircraft were committed during the early morning hours with but little success—the situation on the ground was so confused that accurate bombing and strafing was impossible. At 0930 the Russians penetrated Berestovaya from the west and at noon the regimental commander gave the 2d Battalion permission to withdraw from the village. However, with the arrival shortly thereafter of reinforcements and five assault guns, the battalion was able to withstand Russian pressure until 1600, when Russian infantry, together with a few tanks, made a fresh attack along the road. The Germans lost two strong points near Hill 676 as the Russians broke through. With the aid of the reserve battalion and the assault guns, the 2d Battalion was able to throw the Russians back. By midnight the 2d Battalion's MLR was restored, but contact had been lost between the 3d and 1st Battalions, the latter having taken up a new defensive position close to the railroad embankment.

At dawn on the 27th the Russians launched an attack fully as powerful as that of the preceding day. Striking from the gap between the 1st and 3d Battalions, a strong infantry force supported by at least 20 tanks attacked the 1st Battalion's positions along the railroad embankment. The battalion's eight 37-mm. antitank guns on the embankment were ineffectual against the Russian T34 tanks and were soon knocked out, whereupon the Germans were forced to give up the embankment.

Toward 1100, after a strong artillery preparation, Russian

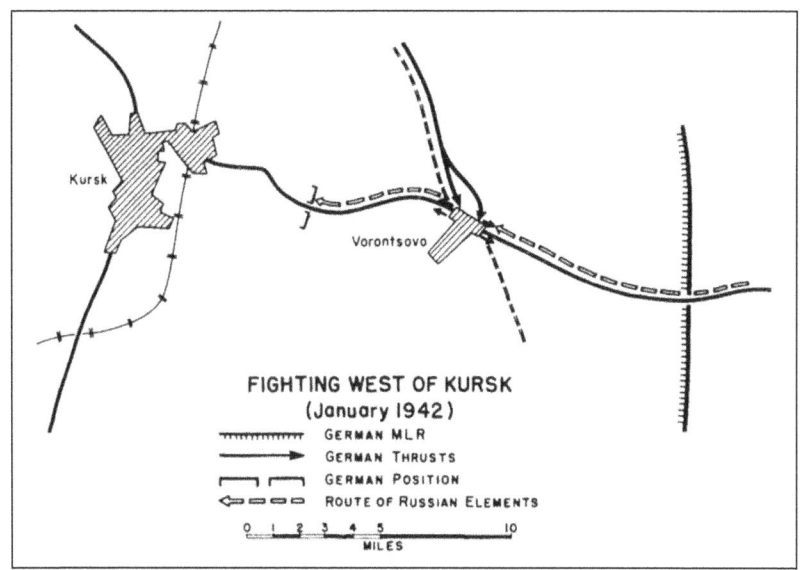

FIGHTING WEST OF KURSK (January 1942)

infantry with tank support attacked from the area just west and northwest of Berestovaya and succeeded in reaching the center of the village. The Germans then counterattacked and recaptured it, following which another Russian force enveloped it by sweeping around the south side.

At 1400, a Russian infantry force, accompanied by several tanks, broke into Berestovaya from the west. Shortly afterward a tank-infantry force attacked along the Lisichansk-Belogorovka road and entered the village from the east. The commander of the 2d Battalion then ordered the evacuation of Berestovaya during the night.

The night withdrawal was carried out without interference. The Russians, who had suffered heavy losses, continued to attack the next day, but were so weak that the Germans had no difficulty in stopping any attempt to advance.

This action exemplifies the tenacity with which both parties fought for villages or other permanent-type shelter during the bitter winter of 1941-42. The German defense of Berestovaya was facilitated by the existence of stone houses, which were not as easily destroyed as the usual Russian structures of wood, clay, or straw.

Throughout the course of their repeated attacks the Russians dissipated their offensive strength without forming points of main effort. Tanks were employed exclusively in support of infantry, a characteristic often evident during the first few months of the war. The Russians could have seized Berestovaya with much less effort if they had tried to envelop it from the beginning. An early Russian thrust to the dominating terrain of Hill 728 would have isolated the German forces in and around Berestovaya and made a prolonged defense impossible.

SEESAW BATTLE IN SUBZERO TEMPERATURES (JANUARY 1942)

By General-Major Burkhart Mueiler-Hillebrand, General-Major Heilmuth Reinhardt, and others

The beginning ascendancy of Russian armor over its German counterpart is exemplified in the following action, during which the Russian tank units showed themselves more aggressive than usual. In January 1942 the German front near Kursk ran north and south about 20 miles east of the city. Because of heavy snowfall cross-country movements was hampered by deep drifts, and temperatures dropped to -30° F. as sharp winds swept across the rolling countryside.

Since there were no woods in the area, visibility was good, except in low places. The monotony of the landscape was relieved only by a number of villages and towns.

Exposed for the first time to the rigors of a Russian winter, the Germans struggled desperately against the elements, as their tanks, trucks, and automatic weapons broke down in the bitter cold. Timber for the improvement of the positions was scarce; accordingly the exhausted German infantry units, then employed along broad sectors, concentrated their defense in village strong points.

The Russians, taking advantage of their numerical superiority and greater experience under winter conditions, sought to undermine the German defense by a series of local, limited-objective attacks.

In the sector of the German 16th Motorized Infantry Division, Russian reconnaissance patrols had skillfully identified a weak spot at the boundary between two regiments. A combined arms team of Russian armor and infantry succeeded in breaking through the German MLR where it crossed the east-west road leading to Kursk, through which a railway and highway vital to German supply movements ran parallel to the front.

Exploiting the breakthrough, a force of about 25 T34 tanks with infantry mounted on them drove on toward Kursk and easily captured the communities in its path which were held solely by German service units. The Russian thrust continued into the next day, when it was stopped about 5 miles from Kursk by a hastily assembled German force. Several attempts to close the gap in the MLR with weak local reserves failed, and the Russians were able to follow up their tank force with two or three battalions of infantry, including some mounted in trucks.

The town of Vorontsovo, situated on the road leading to Kursk, was occupied by a weak Russian force. A German tank battalion, whose tank strength had fallen to 22, was released from another sector and sent in from the north against the right flank of the breakthrough force. The battalion took Vorontsovo by a coup de main, whereupon the Russians had to discontinue their westward advance.

After receiving meager reinforcements in the form of one 88-mm. antiaircraft gun and a battalion of infantry replacements that had just arrived from the zone of interior, the Germans conducted harassing raids in the areas east and west of Vorontsovo, effectively interfering with the supply of those Russian troops that had been cutoff west of the town. On the third day of the action these isolated Russian forces attacked with infantry and tanks but were repulsed.

On the following day, during a driving snowstorm, the Russians attacked Vorontsovo from both the east and west, the thrust from the west being supported by tanks. Taking advantage of their greater ground clearance and lower ground pressure, the Russian tanks swept across terrain that the Germans had considered impassable for armor.

The young German infantry replacements, untested in battle,

lacked experience in hand-to-hand fighting in villages and towns. They had not yet learned to fight in conjunction with tanks and were quickly overcome. Inferior in fire power and mobility to their Russian opposites, the German tanks were almost completely wiped out, and Vorontsovo was once again in Russian hands.

The Russian attack on this key town from two opposite directions was perfectly coordinated. The Germans never found out whether the two Russian forces had established radio contact or whether, perhaps, they were assisted by civilians who had remained in the town. Executed in a driving snowstorm, the Russian attack achieved surprise because the German precautions were inadequate. Extensive reconnaissance and security measures are elementary precautions that must be taken, regardless of the weather. To be derelict in these essentials is to risk lives.

The German counterattack was inadequately supported and led, and the inexperienced infantry were more a hindrance than a help in the operation. An armored unit on an independent mission must be accompanied by seasoned troops equipped with the necessary supporting weapons.

GERMAN RAID ON A RUSSIAN STRONG POINT IN NORTHERN FINLAND (FEBRUARY 1944)

By General-Major Burkhart Mueiler-Hillebrand, General-Major Heilmuth Reinhardt, and others

During the winter of 1943-44 the XIX Mountain Infantry Corps, occupying the northern sector of the Twentieth Mountain Army, was composed of two mountain divisions and one coastal defense division. The corps was opposed by numerically superior Russian forces. Both the Germans and Russians were holding fairly well-constructed positions for the third successive winter.

One of the two mountain infantry divisions, reinforced by special troops, occupied positions in the rocky tundra terrain about a mile west of the Litsa River, whose course was completely frozen over during the winter and therefore constituted no serious barrier. The tundra region combines the features of subalpine mountain tops and hilly terrain. The relatively minor elevations afford good observation of the intermediate terrain. Bare, rocky ground alternates with mossy patches. With the exception of some scattered, stunted birches the vegetation offers little cover.

The German front line consisted of a chain of unevenly spaced strong points, each organized for all-around defense. In some sectors the intervals between strong points measured up to 1 mile. These gaps were protected by an intricate defense system involving mutual fire support from the strong points and, if necessary, the commitment of local reserves. In general, the MLR was an imaginary line connect-i ng the positions that had been prepared for defensive weapons. Along this line stood sentries, and additional listening posts were manned at night and

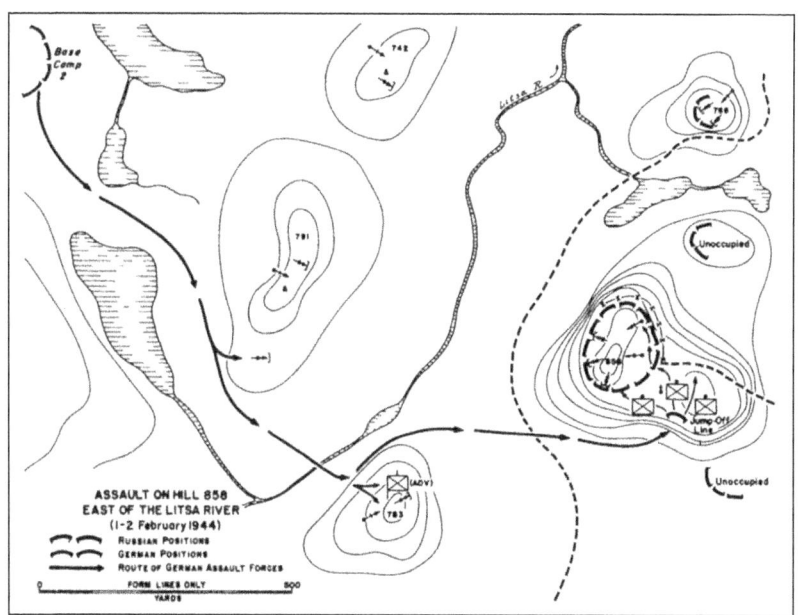

ASSAULT ON HILLl 858 EAST OF LITSA RIVER (1-2 February 1944)

during bad weather. Only during a state of alert were the positions fully occupied. The distance between the German and Russian lines varied between 1,000 yards and 1 mile.

Both sides limited their activities to intensive patrol actions, and operations in greater than squad strength were a rarity during the winter. In addition to the constant close-range reconnaissance, which was essential for security, especially during the long winter nights and during snowstorms, both sides carried out raids and probing attacks to gather information, disrupt supply traffic, and keep intact the aggressiveness of the troops.

Early in January 1944 the 1st Battalion, 143d Mountain Infantry Regiment, received orders to prepare and carry out a raid against the Russian strong point on Hill 858 (map below).

The objective of this raid was to take prisoners and to destroy as many of the enemy defensive installations and shelters as possible. To assure success, the raid was to be preceded by meticulous preparations, for which the battalion was allowed a maximum of four weeks. Hill 858 had been selected because it had not been attacked by the Germans since 1941. The steep western and southern slopes of the hill had been considered insurmountable, especially in winter. The Germans therefore assumed that the Russian garrison, whose outposts controlled the northern and eastern approaches of the hill, felt quite safe in its bastion and would consequently be more liable to relax its guard than troops in other sectors. On the basis of aerial photographs and close reconnaissance it appeared that wire obstacles had been set up only along the northern and eastern perimeter of the strong point. Another factor that influenced the choice of this objective was that German heavy weapons and reserve elements would be able to lend effective support from Hills 742, 791, and 783, which were located in the no man's land between the German strong points and Hill 858.

According to air and ground reconnaissance, the Russian strong point was held by one reinforced platoon. The German battalion commander decided to select a correspondingly small assault force, consisting of 1 platoon sergeant, 3 squad leaders, and 24 men. This force was to be subdivided into an assault squad, composed of the sergeant, 1 squad leader, and 10 men, and 2 supporting squads, each composed of a squad leader and 7 men. The assault force was assisted by reconnaissance elements, a medical team, a machinegun squad with two heavy machineguns, and a mortar squad with one 80-mm. mortar.

The German strong point located closest to the objective was designated Base Camp 2, where one mountain infantry and one engineer platoon were ordered to stand by as reserve forces. Artillery support would be provided upon request.

The raid was to be directed from a forward CP to be established on Hill 783. Between Base Camp 2 and the forward CP contact was to be maintained by telephone and radio. Wire lines would be extended to the assault force's jumpoff line just southeast of the objective. Radio silence was to be imposed during the initial phase of the raid.

Hofer, a battle-tested master sergeant who had proven his ability to lead such raids on previous occasions, was placed in command of the assault squad. He was an excellent mountaineer from the Tyrol and volunteered for this mission. In his mind there was little doubt that, given the right weather and sufficient time for preparation, it would be possible to climb the steep slopes leading to the Russian strong point.

Plans called for the assault squad to be armed exclusively with captured Russian submachineguns, and each man was to carry six magazines of ammunition. The supporting squads were to be equipped with two rifle grenade launchers and 60 grenades, a medium mortar with 48 rounds, and a heavy machinegun with 3,000 rounds. The men were also to carry mines and demolition charges to blow up the Russian installations. In addition, the assault squad was to be issued three Very pistols and flares.

All men were to wear padded winter uniforms and felt boots, except for the members of the assault force, who were to be issued ski boots, whose heavy rubber soles afforded extra traction. Each man was to wear a long white parka with hood, white outer trousers, a woolen cap, and woolen mittens with a hole for the trigger finger. The ammunition was to be carried in outside pockets of their parkas, and a Finnish dagger was to be kept handy. After careful deliberation it was decided not to use skis or wear colored brassards for identification as had been customary on patrol, because speed was less important than remaining unobserved.

The emergency-type rations carried by the assault force was to include combination chocolate-cola candy bars, hardtack, bacon, and dextrose. In addition to the usual supplies, the medical team was to take along a dog sled, two collapsible ski sleds, several reindeer-skin-lined sleeping bags, and some vacuum bottles filled with hot tea.

Before the operation was launched, recently taken aerial

photographs were compared with older ones. Apart from a few hitherto unobserved shelters, they revealed no substantial changes in the Russian dispositions. Each man of the assault force was given an opportunity to familiarize himself with the terrain and the disposition of the Russian outposts by observation from Base Camp 2 and the OP's atop Hills 791 and 742. The information thus obtained was collated and formed the basis for panoramic sketches, which were then studied and evaluated in the light of the most recent aerial photographs.

In the German rear area, terrain features resembling the Russian-held strong point were used by the engineer platoon to build a replica of the Russian installations. For almost 2 weeks the assault force carried out a series of dry runs, some of them with live ammunition. During this intensive training period weapons, clothing, and equipment were tested, as were also the various tactical solutions to achieve perfect coordination among the different elements.

The originally proposed plan of dividing the assault force into three separate squads appeared to be the most effective and was finally adopted. During the approach the assault squad was to be split and each half was to be guided to the jumpoff line by one of the supporting squads. The latter were then to occupy their designated positions on the southern and southeastern slopes of Hill 858, while the assault squad reassembled and prepared to move out. Naturally, every man had to be given precise instructions as to the part he was to take in the raid, the success of which depended on maximum precision in timing.

The battalion commander ordered all participating leaders to attend map exercises, where different phases of the adopted and alternate plans of action were reviewed, including possible enemy counter-measures. The nearest major Russian strong point was 1 mile to the rear of Hill 858, so that the intervention by reserves was not expected less than 45 minutes after an alert had been sounded. The powdery snow, averaging over 3 feet in depth, would prevent these reserves from making better time.

After a prolonged freezing spell, during which the temperatures dipped as low as -40° F., the sky was overcast and toward noon of 1 February light snow flurries began to fall. By evening the flurries turned into a regular snowstorm. This was ideal weather for the execution of the planned raid and, since all preparations had been made and the men were well rested, the assault was set for that night.

At 0030 the raiding party left Base Camp 2. The reconnaissance elements, constituting the point, led the way. Following in sequence were the officer in charge of the operation with headquarters personnel to man the forward CP, the medium mortar squad, the assault force proper, the medical team, and the heavy machinegun squad. Each element kept within sight of the one ahead. Part way up the southern slope of Hill 791 the machinegun squad dropped out and moved to a previously designated point from which it covered the advance of the other elements.

Shortly after the raiding party had set out, the snowstorm let up and presently only a few clouds obscured an otherwise clear, moonlit sky. The improved visibility was expected to be unfavorable for the execution of the raid. However, the raiding party continued its march, knowing that once the moon was down, visibility would again be poor. Despite the excellent visibility for the Russians, Hill 783 was reached safely at 0115. As soon as the command post had been established and sentries posted, the assault force proceeded on toward Hill 858. By 0300 the moon had set, and soon thereafter, despite the deep snow and occasional Russian flares, the assault force arrived at the foot of Hill 858, apparently without being observed. Over the steepest portion of the hill's slope the men had to crawl and climb in two single files, a feat that required great effort and skill.

By 0345 all the men were assembled in the jumpoff line. The two supporting squads took up their assigned positions without making contact with the enemy. Hofer and his squad began to work their way toward the road leading to the objective from the east. Concealed by the snow that was banked high on both sides of the road, Hofer hoped to gain access to the Russian compound. When he reached a point about 40 yards from the communication trench that connected the various shelters and emplacements, Hofer saw a Russian emerging from a shelter and walking toward the northeastern part of the compound. Without having noticed the Germans, the Russian disappeared in another section of the trench. Without hesitation Hofer decided to capture the bunker. Just as his squad was getting ready for the assault, Hofer discovered that he had mistaken a stone-reinforced section of the trench for a bunker. He quickly changed his mind, regrouped his squad, and advanced in the direction of the shelters at the northeast end of the compound by moving along the communication trench. One of his men noticed a cable lying in the trench and cut it. Suddenly the squad leader heard the steps of a man coming toward him in the dark. At a given signal the Germans pounced on him and overpowered him,. While the squad leader and his men were trying to hold down the struggling Russian in the narrow trench, a second Russian approached unobserved. He saw the scuffle and, shouting for help, made a dash for the nearest shelter before any German could stop him. Since these shouts were bound to alert the Russian garrison and since he had at least captured one prisoner Hofer decided to pull his men back at once and leave the neutralization of the strong point installations to heavy weapons and artillery fire. With the information he had obtained, he would be able to pinpoint their targets.

The withdrawal took place according to plan. First the assault squad evacuated the area taking along the prisoner, then the supporting squad on the left, and finally the one on the right abandoned their positions. The supporting squad on the left did not have time to mine the communication trench and thereby obstruct it as intended. The Russians who had emerged from their shelters on the double were pinned down by grenade launcher and submachinegun fire from the German rear guard, which inflicted heavy losses before following the main body. Hofer was the last man to leave the hill.

As soon as the Russians realized that the Germans were pulling out, they recovered from the initial shock and began to fire light and medium mortars in' the presumed direction of the German withdrawal. Since the Russians were unaware of the route the Germans had taken, their fire missed the single-file column retracing its steps down Hill 858.

At 0440 the assault force reached a point about midway between Hills 858 and 783. The sergeant fired a red flare, which both indicated his position and requested fire on Hill 858. The Germans on the surrounding hills were just waiting for this signal. With sudden vehemence the prepared fire of combined heavy weapons and artillery was unleashed, thus facilitating the further withdrawal of the assault force. The Russians also fired flares and lit up the no man's land between the German and Russian strong points with long-burning signal rockets. In addition to the Russian mortars firing from Hill 858, heavy machineguns on Hill 766 now joined in and raked the Litsa Valley. Their fire was well adjusted and German counterfire failed to silence them. The Russian mortars also directed well-aimed projectiles on Base Camp 2.

The withdrawing assault force took advantage of every terrain feature while traversing the northern slope of Hill 783 and crossing the Litsa. Up to that point it had not suffered a single casualty. When it was moving up the slope of Hill 791 from the bottom of Litsa Valley, the end of the column was suddenly hit by a hail of machinegun fire from Hill 766. Five men were wounded and, when a 120-mm. mortar shell scored a direct hit on the machinegun squad on the south slope of Hill 791, the Germans suffered six additional casualties.

The last elements of the assault force reached Base Camp 2 at 0530, by which time all the wounded had been brought back safely and given first aid. Fifteen minutes later the Germans ceased firing and the Russians followed suit soon afterward.

This action is typical of the small-scale fighting that took place in northern Finland from 1941 through 1944. Meticulous preparations and painstaking efforts usually led to negligible results. In this instance the German raiders did achieve surprise and were able to capture a prisoner, but they found out that the Russians on Hill 858 were on the alert, despite the fact that this strong point had not been attacked in 3 years. Interrogation of the prisoner provided little information, except that the garrison on the hill had recently been relieved by fresh troops. If a lesson was to be learned from this raid, it was that even the most careful preparation could not guarantee the success of such an operation.

MORALE DURING WINTER

From German Winter Warfare, US War Department

a. General

The coming winter will again severely tax the spiritual stamina of the soldier. All suitable means commensurate with the situation and combat conditions will be employed to bolster his inner resilience. The example of the soldier, especially the officer who has proved himself in all situations, is a determining factor in maintaining the morale of the troops. Eagerness for action and good discipline must be maintained, especially behind the lines. Prerequisites in assuring morale are consideration for the welfare of troops, tolerable shelter, and adequate provisions. Winter equipment, lighting facilities, and fuel must be procured in advance or substitutes provided. Important! Stimulate the initiative of troops. Shows should be staged and soldiers encouraged to participate in them. Intelligent organization of spare time is the best means of preventing useless brooding, rumor-mongering, and disciplinary offenses.

The welfare of troops in the lines has priority. Morale-building supplies for the front must actually reach the front lines. There must be no pigeonholing in depots, railroad stations, headquarters, or orderly rooms. Checks against delay must be made continually. Commanders and headquarters must be in constant communication with field offices of the High Command of the Armed Forces.

b. Recreational Aids

(1) READING MATERIAL.

Do not leave newspapers lying around. Newspapers, bulletins, and magazines must reach the front fast. There the soldier is waiting for recent news. Papers of occupied territories should be sent forward because they do not have to be transported far.

Front papers of field armies also serve the purpose of inculcating combat doctrine in troops.

Exchange of library kits between battalions and regiments should be encouraged. Field library kits of the Army Book Service (Heeresbücherei) are exclusively for front-line troops. Rear echelons and higher headquarters are normally equipped with Rosenberg libraries.

"Information for Troops" (Mitteilungen für die Truppe) continues to be distributed through the Army Postal Service (Feldpost) to divisions, two copies per unit. Report immediately any failure to receive copies. This also applies to "Information for the Officer Corps" (Mitteilungen für das Offizierkorps).

(2) LECTURES.

Important lectures by speakers from the High Command of the Armed Forces are possible only under quiet conditions and after long preparation. Lectures by members of units on general cultural subjects (history, geography, travel, economics, engineering, fine arts) have been successful even in small units. The units themselves have good men for this purpose!

(3) RADIO.

The Army radio receiving set has worked even in winter on the Eastern Front. The further issue of sets and spare parts, on the basis of current production, is confined to front-line troops and is carried out only through higher signal officers of signal regiments. Production and distribution of additional sets and spare parts is being stressed. Rear installations and welfare organizations are equipped with commercial receivers.

(4) MOVIES.

Theaters are improvised behind the front lines on the basis of experience. The increase of available machines, especially of the projector unit with direct-current generator for localities without power supply, is desirable. Pictures shown are coordinated by the division G-2.

(5) EMPLOYMENT OF "STRENGTH THROUGH JOY" GROUPS.

On the Eastern Front only tours by small acting troupes are ordinarily possible. Transportation and shelter must be considered. When constructing new motion-picture theaters, provide stage facilities for acting troupes. The stages will also be used for official business (lectures, instruction, briefing, schools, etc.). It is important to employ "Strength through Joy" groups (KdF.-Gruppen) according to plan. Provide them with transportation facilities, cooperate with them, pay attention to their welfare, and provide for their security in guerrilla territory.

(6) COMPETITIONS.

Competitions are particularly valuable in all respects. New facilities have been provided for the winter of 1942-43. Important activities in this field are inventions and improvements of arms and equipments.

(7) IMPROVEMENT OF QUARTERS.

The troops should be urged to improve their quarters by their own handiwork. Arts and crafts have a place in the construction of shelters. In view of the bare-minimum shelter conditions in the east, this is particularly important. Encourage by competitions the improvement of quarters, moving-picture halls, theaters, kitchens, storerooms, stables, and gardens.

(8) ORGANIZATION OF SPARE TIME.

In organizing spare time, schools for choir leaders are particularly valuable. Train choir leaders for the units of divisions and regiments. Also encourage hobbies, crafts, and amateur theatrical performances by and for the troops. Occupational aid through correspondence courses and civilian work groups is also successful. This kind of instruction has practical value for the future of the soldier.

(9) SERVICE CENTERS.

Service centers should be especially promoted. Unattractive

living conditions and the lack of "places to go" and restaurants on the Eastern Front must be remembered. The establishment of numerous service centers is necessary. At larger service centers a senior hostess and several junior hostesses of the German Red Cross (DRK) must be assigned.

(10) FRONT CONVALESCENT CAMPS.

These are successful without exception. Convalescent camps behind front lines meet an urgent need of troops. In large areas and broad front sectors the establishment of small convalescent camps for regiments has been successful.

FINNISH TACTICS - SMALL UNITS

*Tactical and Technical Trends,
No. 6, August 27, 1942.*

Introduction.

The tactical doctrine of the Finnish Army presupposes an overwhelming superiority in numbers and materiel on the part of its potential enemy. To increase the effectiveness of their defense against such an enemy, Finnish tactics take advantage of the available natural factors: the characteristics of the Finnish people, and the nature and possibilities of Finland's terrain.

Their long struggle with poor soil caused the Finnish people to develop exceptional physical strength, iron nerves, resourcefulness, and a stubborn will. These traits, together with the high level of popular education, general skill in arms, the expert use of skis, and familiarity with life in the woods make the Finnish soldier especially suited for independent action.

The Finns are naturally uncommunicative, like to go their own way, and are of a suspicious nature. Not easily aroused to enthusiasm, they are strong-willed, and once an idea is conceived it is held tenaciously. Finns are hard to lead, but, once having accepted a leader, are extremely loyal.

The country is largely covered with woods, thousands of lakes, and numerous rivers and swamps. The coastline is very irregular. Travel must be confined to roads since crosscountry communication is almost impossible. The roads are many miles apart and hemmed in by the forest. The clearings for agricultural purposes are few and small. It is a rolling country, with very few marked elevations.

Finns realized long ago that if war came to them, it would be a defensive conflict begun by an aggressor and fought from the very first day within their own boundaries. The general plan of defense assumes that the enemy will be unprepared by nature and experience to cope with conditions in Finland.

General.

Although Finnish troops are organized into divisions, brigades, regiments, etc., in the same manner as other modern armies, their operations against an enemy emphasize use of small units: patrols, attacking groups, and detachments.

The basic tactical doctrine assumes that the enemy will follow avenues of approach which will make him vulnerable to encirclement, after which his forces are to be destroyed piecemeal. This is accomplished by forcing the enemy to follow routes outlined by either natural or artificial obstacles until he reaches the terrain selected for his annihilation.

The tactics of annihilation are carried out through the use of a "motti". In original usage the word motti means a pile of sawn timber held in position by upright stakes driven in at intervals along its edges. In military usage, motti refers to an enemy group surrounded by Finnish patrols each of from eight to twelve men armed with automatic arms. Lines of communication are severed and the surrounded enemy is decimated by numerous raids, severe cold, and slow starvation. This encirclement may last several months, until the enemy force is completely destroyed.

A modern army invading Finland is to a large extent confined to the roads in order to move its mechanized units and weapons forward. Finnish light artillery is so emplaced as to force these moving columns off the road into the adjacent forests. The Finns then rush their machine guns and antitank guns through the forest on a special type of sled called a "pulka"; they attack and are off again before the enemy can take any counteraction.

Finnish winter uniforms are made of white skins and furs, and patrols wear a white cape with a hood attached. Against a snow-covered background they are almost invisible to the enemy.

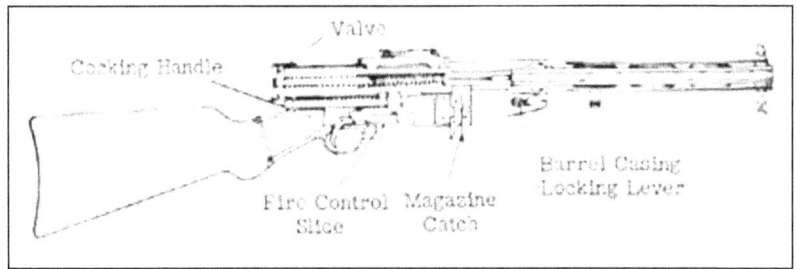

9-MM. MACHINE CARBINE - SUOMI

Materiel is also camouflaged to blend with the white background. For example, the Finns cover captured tanks with lime-wash to make them less conspicuous.

No Finnish unit, however small, is ever sent out upon operations of more than a few hours' length without heating equipment adapted to its needs. Dugouts are constructed, lined with skins and roofed with birch logs capable of supporting several feet of snow. In each of these shelters there is a stove designed to burn without sparks or visible trace of smoke.

The Finns are experts on skis and rely mainly on their use in winter; material is transported on motor trucks, horse-drawn sleighs, and dog-team sleds. Ski troops have been known to travel over 65 miles a day.

The chief offensive weapon of the Finns is the Suomi machine carbine, similar to our sub-machine gun (see sketch). Ordinary Central European military tactics demands fire beginning at long ranges in the form of artillery preparation and increasing gradually in intensity over a considerable period of time. Something entirely different is required for warfare in the Finnish woods. Here the weapons must be located far forward and maximum fire power attained immediately. This demands an automatic weapon which is light and mobile. This weapon must be unusually well-balanced to ensure good aim under difficulties incident to forest fighting. The Suomi carbine is the weapon which fulfills all these requirements.

Long-range rifles are not suitable for forest warfare because

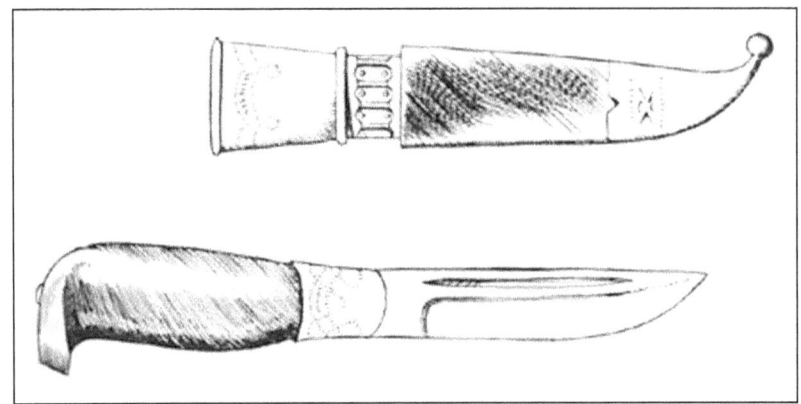
FINNISH "PUUKKO"

of the very limited fields of fire.

In Finnish practice, the place of the bayonet is taken by the "puukko" (see sketch). The best puukko, or Finnish knife, comes from Lapland. It usually has a straight blade 7 1/2 in. long, tapering to a point in the last 1 1/2 in. Its handle is 4 1/2 in. long and made of polished wood. It is generally enclosed in a scabbard of tooled leather. The puukko is a weapon for the silence and darkness of the woods. It is carried by most Finnish troops and particularly adapted to night raids.

Activities of Patrols.

Against massed troops and columns of the enemy, Finnish patrols employ fire from automatic weapons, trench mortars, and light artillery. However, columns are annihilated chiefly by swift movement and automatic fire. For this purpose ski troops are held in readiness and are put into action at the proper time. These ski troops attack a column on the flank, move rapidly along the whole length, and inflict casualties with automatic weapons.

When decisive action is expected to take place in woods, machine guns, as a rule, are not taken along. These have little effect in woods and may easily fall into the hands of the enemy. On the other hand, the Finns recognize the fact that fire of lighter automatic weapons increases the momentum of attack in the woods and employ them in unusually large numbers.

The Finns do not attack large bodies of enemy troops. They devote energies primarily to three specialized tasks: a) depriving the enemy divisions of their command by attacking and destroying regimental and brigade headquarters; b) concentrating on the destruction of the field-kitchens; and c) attacking communications.

When the enemy lines of communication are extended, they are subjected to incessant harassing. For this purpose detachments of picked ski-runners are considered most suitable.

A condition for success of the raid is that such detachments receive clear, and very often detailed instructions. Orders to such detachments must therefore be issued by an experienced officer, either a battalion or regimental commander.

During very cold weather, night attacks yield better results against hostile troops if these have had to halt in the open for lack of suitable bivouacs. The mere fact that the activities of patrols and aircraft prevent the enemy from lighting fires causes many frostbites and severe colds, and makes him more vulnerable to attacks by major forces. Patrols are equipped with machine carbines, hand grenades, and materiel for destroying armored vehicles and for burning trains, supplies, etc.

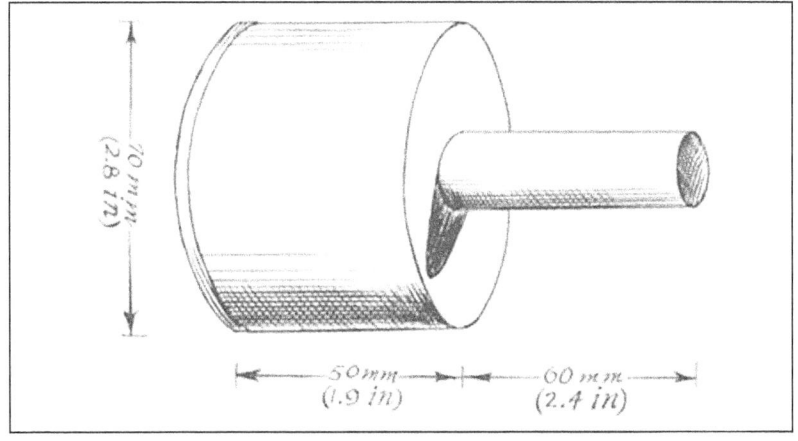

FINNISH "PARTISAN INCENDIARY GRENADE"

In addition to inflicting direct casualties, patrol activity creates a feeling of uncertainty among enemy troops and forces them to take excessive measures of precaution. For example, as a result of such activity by Finnish patrols, the commander of a Russian tank corps ordered an entire tank brigade to reconnoiter the terrain far to the rear of the Russian positions.

For the destruction of armored vehicles, and for burning trains, Finnish patrols are provided with "partisan incendiary grenades" (see sketch on previous page). These contain about 300 grams of thermite. Arming is effected by striking the friction surface of a match box against the friction surface at the end of the handle. By means of a fuse card the thermite is ignited 5 or 6 seconds later.

Antitank Defense.

During the first Russo-Finnish War (1939) great losses were suffered by Russian tank units attempting to penetrate Finnish antitank defenses.

The first Russian attempt to attack with tanks was stopped and disorganized by fields of mines arranged inside the frontier. The mines were placed on all the roads, paths, and bridges, and caused severe losses among the tanks.

These mines were not placed in fixed positions. During the night Finnish patrols would replace destroyed mines, particularly on roads over which some Russian units had already passed. Many tanks were destroyed in this way.

In order to prevent the removal of mines by the enemy, mine fields are kept under constant observation and are covered by infantry fire.

The Finns construct tank obstacles of various types, and mine the weaker points in the lay-out of obstacles. One of these obstacles is an abatis. An abatis is at least 30 yards in depth and made of trees with trunks measuring over 8 inches in diameter. Trees are cut from 3 to 4 feet above the ground but left attached to their stumps. The tops are pointed toward the defender. The trees are attached to one another with steel wire, large nails, or hooks, and barbed wire is interlaced in all directions. With traps inside such barriers, their removal is rendered very difficult. The tops of these trees must not be parallel but should partly cross one another so as not to allow passage between the trunks.

Antitank defense companies are employed for destruction of tanks which may break through the main line of resistance. Such missions require alert and aggressive men.

The antitank defense company consists of 3 platoons of 4 sections each; a section includes a leader, an assistant leader, 5 men, 3 men in reserve. The company is equipped with several cargo trucks for various types of mines and Molotov cocktails.

The company performs on the principle that observation from a tank is limited and that it cannot fire at an object within a radius of 3 to 4 yards. A section operates in the following manner:

Men are placed in pairs, one on each side of the road over a distance of 75 to 100 yards. Each man digs a shelter for himself and thoroughly camouflages it. Tanks, which generally drive along the road in platoons of 5 vehicles each, are allowed to advance to a point where the first tank is abreast of the last pair of men. Here it is destroyed by a mine drawn across the road in its path. This is usually a signal for the other pairs of men to take advantage of the resultant confusion and simultaneously destroy the other tanks. To accomplish the destruction of such a tank group, terrain is selected where it is difficult for the tanks to leave the road, as in dense woods or on stony ground.

A mine drawn across the road is constructed of four ordinary tank mines coupled together with wire, the distance between each mine being about 1 inch. A wire about 25 yards long is attached to each end of the series of mines, and by means of this wire they are drawn across the road. The parts of the wire lying on the road are camouflaged. Since the bottom of the mine is indented and does not slide easily, a plank or strip of tin must be placed underneath. As the tank approaches, the mines are drawn onto the road in front of it.

Stopping of the first tank in the column is the signal for a general attack. An antitank mine is thrown in front of the track of each tank and combustible bottles are thrown simultaneously. Immediately after the detonation of the antitank mine and the immobilization of the tank, a grenade thrower jumps or climbs onto the tank and throws a hand grenade through the roof shutter of the turret.

The audacity of antitank defense personnel can best be illustrated by reports of their action north of Lake Ladoga against Russian tanks. Lacking other tank-destroying equipment, Finnish soldiers were reported to have bent the barrels of the tank machine guns by hitting them with trunks of birch trees.

Antitank defense platoons cooperate with the antitank gun platoons whenever possible. When the latter hit a tank they signal the antitank defense personnel to destroy it.

Possessing very few antitank guns, the Finns became experts in the accurate delivery of fire, and strategic emplacement. They realized that antitank guns located on the main line of resistance are destroyed either by the fire of hostile tank guns or by being overrun by attacking tanks. Finnish tactics stress that antitank guns, when possible, should be located on reverse slopes, on ground interspersed with boulders, under cover of terrain difficult to pass, or under protection of mines placed well forward. A frequent change of positions is also a method of avoiding destruction.

Their best defense against air attacks, and one utilized to great advantage by Finnish troops, is the natural cover and concealment afforded by local terrain. Thick forests and the excellent camouflage of troops and materiel make air observation very difficult.

In addition to the use of basic infantry weapons on enemy aircraft, the Finns employ the 76-mm., 40-mm., and 20-mm.

antiaircraft guns and the 7.62-mm. antiaircraft machine gun. Of these, the 40-mm. antiaircraft gun proved to be the most efficient in the ratio of ammunition expended to the number of planes downed. Small-arms antiaircraft fire is delivered only by platoons.

It has been reported that during the Russo-Finnish War, the Finns found the use of Stokes mortars effective against dive-bombing attacks. The mortars were placed in batteries of four, under the command of an officer. The future position of the target was estimated by the gunners. Mortar shells were kept ready at charges 1, 2, and 3. The officer selected the charge and gave the initial order to fire. Although the number of planes brought down by this method was not great, the fire interfered with the aim of the bombers and kept them at a respectful distance. This expedient was originally improvised by infantry units which had no other means of antiaircraft defense.

COMBAT IN HIGH MOUNTAINS, SNOW, AND EXTREME COLD

From Intelligence Bulletin, July 1943

Official German military doctrine dealing with the tactics to be used in high mountains and under conditions of extreme cold is summarized in this section. The information has been extracted from German Army documents.

1. IN HIGH MOUNTAINS

A. COMMAND

The German Army emphasizes that the skill and leadership of junior commanders are severely tested in mountain warfare inasmuch as forces will generally be split into relatively small groups. The efficient handling of these groups demands a high standard of training and discipline. Columns will often be separated by wide areas of difficult country, and, since lateral communication is often very difficult, command of deployed units becomes much more complicated than during operations over ordinary terrain.

B. MOVEMENT

(1) The Germans recognize that the limited number of trails and the tendency of men and animals to become exhausted have a decisive influence on movement.

(2) Units are divided into numerous marching groups, none of which is larger than a reinforced company, a gun battery, or an engineer platoon. The Germans maintain that in this way the danger of ambush can be overcome, and each group can fight independently.

(3) Engineers are well forward (with protective patrols) to help repair roads.

(4) Aware that small enemy forces can hold up the advance of a whole column, the Germans consider it necessary to have

single guns well forward. They also regard flank protection as very important; for this reason stationary, as well as mobile, patrols are used.

(5) When unusually steep stretches are encountered, infantry troops [probably reserves] move forward and disperse themselves among the pack animals of the artillery, for the purpose of helping the artillery in an emergency.

(6) Pack artillery moves at march pace (2 1/2 miles per hour) and after marches of over 6 hours, 3 to 4 hours rest is necessary. Short halts are considered useless, because men and animals must be able to unload.

(7) The Germans stipulate that for every 325 yards ascent or 550 yards descent, 1 hour should be added to the time which would be estimated necessary to cover the same map distance on ordinary terrain.

C. SUPPLIES

(1) The supply echelon may include some, or all, of the following means of transport: motor vehicles (with preference given to vehicles of from 1 to 2 tons), horse- and mule-drawn vehicles, rope railways, pack animals, and manpower. Transport aviation may also be used if the terrain permits.

(2) The Germans have found that a cart drawn by two small horses can be highly practical in mountainous country.

(3) The German Army stresses that supplies must initially be packed in containers suitable for pack transport, in order to avoid a waste of time in repacking en route.

(4) Man loads vary from 45 to 75 pounds.

(5) In general, supplies are organized into valley columns and mountain columns. Valley columns carry supplies for 2 days, and mountain columns carry supplies for 1 to 2 days.

D. WEAPONS

(1) Light machine guns are used more often than heavy machine guns.

(2) Mortars are used extensively, and often replace light artillery.

(3) Antitank guns and heavy machine guns are mostly used for covering road blocks.

(4) It is a German principle that effectiveness of artillery fire from valleys depends on the careful selection of observation posts, and on efficient communication between these posts and single gun positions. "It cannot be overemphasized," the Germans say, "how difficult it is for artillery to leave the roads or level ground."

(5) In general, the emphasis is on the lighter weapons.

E. RECONNAISSANCE

Apart from normal reconnaissance tasks, it is considered important to mark trails to show: which areas can be observed by the opposition, how far pack transport can be used, where trails need improving, and where troops must assume the responsibility of carrying everything themselves.

F. SIGNALS

(1) The Germans use radio as the primary means of communication, because of the great difficulty of laying lines.

(2) Motorcycles and bicycles are used in the valleys.

(3) The Germans take into account the fact that lateral communication is often very difficult and sometimes impossible.

G. ENGINEERS

German engineers in mountain units are assigned the following tasks in addition to their normal duties: bridging swift mountain streams, clearing mule trails, and constructing rope and cable railways.

H. ATTACK TACTICS

(1) Attacks across mountains usually have the subsidiary missions of protecting the flanks of the main attack (usually made through a valley), working around the rear of the

opposition, or providing flanking fire for the main attack.

(2) It is a German axiom that the early possession of commanding heights is essential to the success of forces moving along the valleys.

(3) Generally, the German main attack follows the line of valleys, which alone gives a certain freedom of movement to a strong force and the necessary supply echelons.

(4) German troops attacking uphill are always on guard against falling rocks and possible landslides caused by supporting artillery fire.

(5) The Germans have found that attacking downhill, while easier for forward troops, often presents tactical and ballistic problems for the artillery.

I. DEFENSE TACTICS

(1) German officers are reminded that defense of any large area of mountainous country ties down a very considerable number of troops.

(2) The Germans believe that if a crest is to be defended, it is better to have only the outpost position on the crest or forward slope and to have the main line of resistance, with heavy weapons, on the reverse slope.

J. TRAINING

(1) In general, the basic training of German mountain troops is that of normal infantry units. Specialized training comes later.

(2) Battalion officers are trained mountain guides, and must pass tests annually.

(3) All guides are required to be expert at map reading and the use of altimeters, at judging weather conditions, at recognizing dangers peculiar to mountainous country, and at overcoming great terrain difficulties in order to reach observation posts.

(4) The necessity for noiseless movement is emphasized,

German crawler tractor, Russia, January 1944

inasmuch as under certain conditions sound may travel farther in mountainous terrain than in open country.

(5) It is stressed that ammunition must be used economically.

(6) Since troops are likely to be separated from their units for a number of days, the Germans require a high standard of discipline and physical toughness.

2. IN SNOW AND EXTREME COLD
A. MOVEMENT

(1) Marching.—The Germans consider it important that clothing should not be too warm. Weapons are covered. Advance guards are strong, and heavy weapons and artillery are well forward. Antitank weapons are distributed along the column. Ski and sleigh troops may be sent out to guard the flanks. Plenty of towing ropes are loaded on motor transport, and horse-drawn and hand-drawn sleighs are considered very useful for transporting weapons and supplies.

(2) Halts.—In contrast with normal German practice in mountains, halts are short when the temperature is very low. Motor transport vehicles are placed radiator to radiator. Snow is cleared under the vehicles, and some sort of foundation is provided for the wheels.

(3) Restrictions.—The Germans limit the use of the tanks and motorized units when the temperature is lower than 5 degrees above zero (Fahrenheit). Motorcycles are considered useless when the snow is more than 8 inches deep. Snow is regarded as a tank obstacle when it is higher than the ground clearance of the tank's belly. German tractors can negotiate snow up to 1 foot in depth; at 1 foot the use of snow-clearing apparatus becomes necessary. At very low temperatures, gasoline consumption is reckoned at five times the normal rate. Snow deeper than 1 foot 4 inches is considered impassable for pack animals.

B. WEAPONS

The German Army warns its mountain troops that:
(1) Distances are usually underestimated in clear weather and overestimated in fog and mist.
(2) At low temperatures weapons often fire short at first.
(3) Ammunition expenditure tends to rise very sharply when visibility is bad.

C. RECONNAISSANCE

When German reconnaissance units are operating in mountains under conditions of extreme cold, extra tasks include obtaining information about the depth of snow, the load capacity of ice surfaces, and the danger of landslides and avalanches.

Regarding direction signs, the Germans warn that the opposition will use every possible form of deception, and that great care must be taken in interpreting the direction of trails correctly. It is acknowledged that there is an ever-present danger of being diverted into an ambush or a strongly defended position.

The usual German methods of indicating trails are to mark trees and rocks, erect poles, and set up flags on staffs. Stakes are used to denote the shoulders of roads.

D. SIGNALS

It is noted that a greater length of time is needed for laying communication wire under mountain conditions, and that cold and dampness lowers the efficiency of a great deal of signal equipment.

E. ATTACK TACTICS

(1) Because of the difficulty of movement, assembly areas are nearer the opposition than is normally the case.
(2) Limited objectives are the rule.
(3) Because deployment is so difficult, it is often delayed until contact has been made.
(4) Combined frontal and flank attacks are used wherever possible.
(5) Commanding positions are considered of added value and are occupied by mobile troops as quickly as possible.
(6) Decentralization of weapons is authorized so that units can deal with surprise attacks without delay.
(7) Attacks are often made by ski troops.

F. DEFENSE TACTICS

German mountain troops are taught that under conditions of snow and extreme cold:

(1) Obstacles take much longer to build.
(2) Strong outposts are highly valuable because they force the opposition to undertake an early deployment.
(3) The usefulness of snow as protection against fire is often overestimated.
(4) Heavy snowfalls render mines useless.

WINTER FLYING PROBLEMS
From Intelligence Bulletin, February 1943

1. RUNWAYS

From numerous experiences during the winters of 1940 and 1941, the German Air Force has found that the maximum efficiency in winter operations is attained by using wheeled landing gear as long as conditions permit. Such use requires immediate rolling of the runways after any appreciable snowfall.

Where heavy snowfalls are expected, the runways are marked off in advance with relation to the prevailing wind direction, so that rolling can be started as soon as the snow is about 2 inches deep. The runways should be laid out to avoid take-offs over mounds of snow or other irregularities of ground and to eliminate as much as possible the necessity of making crosswind landings.

Snow fences must be erected as a protection against drifts. If the direction of the prevailing wind coincides with that of the runway, the fences are set at an angle of about 25 to 30 degrees to the wind in order to deflect the snow outwards. It is especially important to place fences at the intersection and at the ends of the runways, and to erect suitable warning markers on all obstacles caused by such work.

Rolling should be carried out continuously to prevent the formation of dangerous snow heaps, and the rolled surface subsequently raked to minimize ice formation. Taxi aprons, as well as main and auxiliary runways, should be kept clear of snow as long as possible.

2. SKIS

The change-over from wheels to skis (see sketch overleaf) is usually made when the unrolled snow has reached a depth of one-third of the diameter of the aircraft wheels. When the snow

German Aircraft on Skis.

is deeper, landing on wheels is possible without risk of turning over, but take-off is prevented by the high rolling resistance of the snow. During this period, special take-off sledges are used. These become detached as the aircraft rises, enabling the plane to land on wheels.

To safeguard the undercarriage as much as possible, landings and take-offs with skis should always be made on snow which has not been rolled. Aircraft on skis must be taxied only on snow-covered surfaces. Taxiing over snow mounds and slopes with sharp drops should be avoided because the skis have a limited range of deflection. As ski-equipped airplanes have a dangerous tendency to ground-loop in cross winds when taxiing on ice or rolled snow surface, extreme care should be taken to keep them from swinging. Multi-engine aircraft may be taxied by the use of either outboard engine, but small curves cause high stresses in the undercarriage and must be avoided. There are no brakes on skis, since on deep soft snow the length of the landing run is shorter than with unbraked wheels.

The normal length of take-off may be expected when the snow is frozen and the temperature below zero, but in warmer temperatures the friction coefficients may become very high, necessitating a longer run. If conditions are so unfavorable that it is impossible to take off, a runway may be created in the snow by taxiing to and fro repeatedly. The take-off run may be interrupted without danger, since an airplane on skis comes to a standstill quickly if the engine is throttled. On the take-off, the handling of aircraft with skis is the same as for those equipped with wheels.

From the point of view of flying, there has been no difficulty in operating the various types of aircraft with skis attached, although speed and general effectiveness are reduced between 5 and 15 percent. However, single engine flight with a Ju 88 so equipped is not possible, and an He 111 with skis can barely maintain level flight on one engine. The same principles apply to the landing run as to the take-off, except in night landings. Light is reflected in the direction of flight by flat expanses of snow on the field, which makes judgment as to altitude impossible, unless the surface has been walked on or ashes have been sprinkled to cut the glare and provide identification marks.

The aircraft must not be allowed to come to a stand-still upon landing, but must be taxied immediately to a previously prepared parking place, equipped with suitable wooden parking gratings which have been smeared with a graphite paste or used engine oil so that the skis will slide over them. Multi-engine aircraft, because of their size, require at least 10 parking gratings while single-engine planes need only about 4. The space between parked aircraft fitted with skis must be twice as great as for those with wheels, because it is not always possible to taxi accurately with skis.

The aircraft are placed on parking gratings so that they will not freeze to the ground. If the bottoms of the tires should become frozen, they must not be forcibly freed but can be loosened either by applying salt, saltwater, or hot air, or by inserting a wire between the tire and the ground. Skis should not be loosened by pushing the fuselage backward and forward, because no undercarriage can stand the strain. Light aircraft may be freed by shaking the wings, with the engine at full throttle. Heavy planes must be jacked up so that wooden gratings can be pushed under each ski. If the equipment necessary for this is not available, the snow must be shoveled away until only one-quarter of the ski, at the center, is still standing on snow. It is then possible to release the aircraft with full power by moving the elevator and rudder.

It is not necessary to wax the skis, but after about 10 flying hours the sliding surfaces must be inspected for signs of wear, and light damage to the hard paper or cement covering may be repaired quite easily. As the stresses on the undercarriage are greater with skis than with wheels, all parts must be carefully inspected at least every 20 hours. In case of boat skis, the cover must be freed from snow and ice before the take-off to obtain complete freedom of motion. In milder weather, these skis must be drained of accumulated snow water daily.

Aircraft fitted with skis must never be moved over ground free from snow without using a special dolly or some other device, nor should aircraft be dragged by the tail skid, even when a moving device has been fitted to the main skis.

3. STORAGE PROBLEMS

If it is impossible to heat the main hangars properly, a separate living room, adequately heated, and a warm, well-ventilated storeroom should be provided. The temperature of the storeroom should not fall below 50 degrees Fahrenheit. Ground maintenance equipment, as well as all drums containing lubricating oil and cooling fluid, should be housed under cover if space is available, but at least one transport vehicle, engine heater, and engine starter should be kept ready for immediate use in a warm place. As much gear as possible should also be kept in heated storerooms. Everything left in the open has to be protected from the wind and condensation by use of matting, tarpaulin, or straw.

Rubber covers, inner tubes, and cables become sensitive to kinks and bends at temperatures below -4 degrees Fahrenheit, but elasticity is restored at room temperature. The most satisfactory temperature for the storage of such articles is between 40 and 60 degrees Fahrenheit, as prolonged higher temperatures are detrimental to rubber. Since the capacity of batteries falls off rapidly with extremely cold temperatures, it is essential that they be removed from equipment left in the open and stored in a warm place until needed. They should be kept fully charged as discharged batteries are likely to freeze at temperatures below 32 degrees.

High-pressure containers should be kept under cover and, if possible, not exposed to cold.

Lubricating oil and antifreeze solution must be stored in protected sheds, heated, if possible, with special precautions against penetration of the drums by water, snow, and ice. The containers, with the filler on the top side, should always be placed on wooden blocks, and should be protected against the weather on all sides. If a warm storeroom is not available, it is possible to warm the drums by covering them with a tarpaulin and blowing in hot air from the engine heater. Baking ovens made of stones and heated by a wood fire may also be used to heat the drums.

Lacquers and certain other finishes (known as "airplane dopes") are very sensitive to cold and dampness, but the place where they are stored must not be directly heated because of the danger of fire.

The lighters that are used for marking out landing runways or obstructions have a very short life in low temperatures, and so are stored during the day in a warm room.

4. STARTING COLD MOTORS

When starting aircraft after a snowstorm, or after prolonged inactivity, all drifted snow deposits must be cleared away. The best way to do this is to open the inspection holes, and thaw or blow away the snow. All aircraft engines require some pre-heating, if they have been left in the open when temperatures are below freezing point. At temperatures below -4 degrees Fahrenheit, it is especially difficult to start an engine because the fuel, injected into the cylinder or atomized by the carburetor, condenses on the cold walls of the cylinder and intake pipes and prevents combustion.

The method generally used to heat the engine is to cover it with a heavy canvas hood and force a draft of hot air into the bottom opening. To do this, the Germans use an engine heater (see sketch), which can warm an airplane motor within 15 to 20 minutes, raising the temperature of the engine approximately 50 degrees. This device heats air by passing it over burning vaporized fuel and then blowing it through double-walled canvas tubes into the hood placed around the engine. The blower of this apparatus may be operated by either a gasoline or an electric motor.

The pre-heating of lubricating oil appears to be the main factor in speeding up cold-weather starting. During cold starts, the lubricant becomes easily diluted by the unburned gasoline in the cylinders, and the oil sludge deposited in the engine dissolves. A much larger quantity than usual is carried to the oil filter. For this reason, it is essential that oil be removed and thoroughly cleaned after each long flight. However, if cleaning devices are connected to a rod in the cockpit, the pilot should clean out the filter during flight. The oil coolers and oil lines to engines should be covered with felt or asbestos to keep in heat

German Aircraft Engine-Heating Device.

while the engine is running. The Germans have also been experimenting with the use of acetylene in starting aircraft engines at very low temperatures, but no operational use of this method has yet been reported.

As variable-pitch propellers are subject to freezing, the blades should be placed in take-off position, with a small angle of attack, when the engine is stopped. During cold starts, the pitch of the propellers should be altered several times backwards and forwards by operating the speed control. This insures that the control mechanism and the oil servo-motor become filled with the cold-starting mixture. This also applies to electric, constant-speed propellers, where the pitch-changing mechanism should be operated over as large a range as possible to distribute the grease uniformly over the gears. This prevents the propeller from changing pitch of its own accord. The gear mechanism should be warmed if the air temperature is below -4 degrees Fahrenheit.

To protect the cooling system against frosts, a mixture of 50 percent glycol and 50 percent water is recommended. Any outside openings or vents leading to the instruments should be covered when in flight, so that snow or rain cannot enter the lines and freeze. All control hinges should be covered with a thin oil to prevent the collection of moisture and subsequent locking of control surfaces.

5. ANTIFREEZING METHODS

The Luftwaffe has developed a special anti-ice paste to be used on the wings, turrets, and tail unit when there is danger of icing. However, as this paste causes the camouflage paint on the aircraft to peel off, it is applied only when there is real danger of ice formation.

When the snow is thick, the control surfaces are likely to be damaged on take-offs and landings by pieces of ice. Care must be taken to insure that the fuselage and lower side of the wings and control surfaces are snow- and waterproof, since snow may penetrate into the aircraft and be deposited there. Subsequent freezing may block the controls or the mechanism for retracting and lowering the landing gear. At very low temperatures, too tight control cables may contract enough to tear away from their supports.

Since ordinary bombsights are electrically heated, they are not affected by extreme cold, but the noses of all bombs exposed to the airstream must be treated with anti-ice paste.

To insure satisfactory operation of guns at low temperatures, maintenance must be carefully checked and guns, appliances, and mountings tested before every flight. During prolonged flights at very low temperatures, the guns should be operated at regular intervals to prevent excessive cooling. Muzzle caps should be fitted on all guns so that snow or ice will not enter the mechanism. When Oerlikon "FF" 20-mm fixed cannon are mounted on aircraft operated under winter conditions, they must be equipped with a special recoil spring, as otherwise the gun may stick when it is fired.

SLEDS FOR WINTER WARFARE

Tactical and Technical Trends,
No. 19, February 25th, 1943

German sources reveal the use of sleds (Ackja) by the Finns to meet the problems of winter transport.

A small flat-bottomed boat-shaped sled, the keel of which forms the running surface, is used for the transport of light loads of different kinds: ammunition, rations, radio equipment, wounded, and light weapons. The following types of sled, modelled on the Finnish pattern, have recently been introduced into the German Army:

German Designation	English Equivalent
Schlitten 300 kg	Sled, 660 lbs
Schlitten 500 kg	Sled, 1,100 lbs
Krankenschlitten	Ambulance sled
Schlitten 1,000 kg	Sled, 2,200 lbs
Leichter Ackja	Light Ackja
Boots-Ackja	Boat-type (clinker-built) Ackja
Waffen-Ackja	Weapon-carrying Ackja

a. Description

Ackjas may be constructed either of three-ply wood or of ordinary planks, clinker-built (with planks or plates put on so that one edge of each overlaps the edge of the plate or plank next to it, like clapboards on a house).

(1) PLYWOOD TYPE

An example is shown in the accompanying sketch, figure 1. The various sections of plywood are cut out, partly shaped by soaking in water, and nailed or riveted into position. The stern of the sled is braced by a 3/4-inch-thick wooden batten secured at each end by strips of 1/64-inch strap iron. Dimensions and design are varied to suit the purpose for which the sled is built, but in every case the sled should be as light as possible.

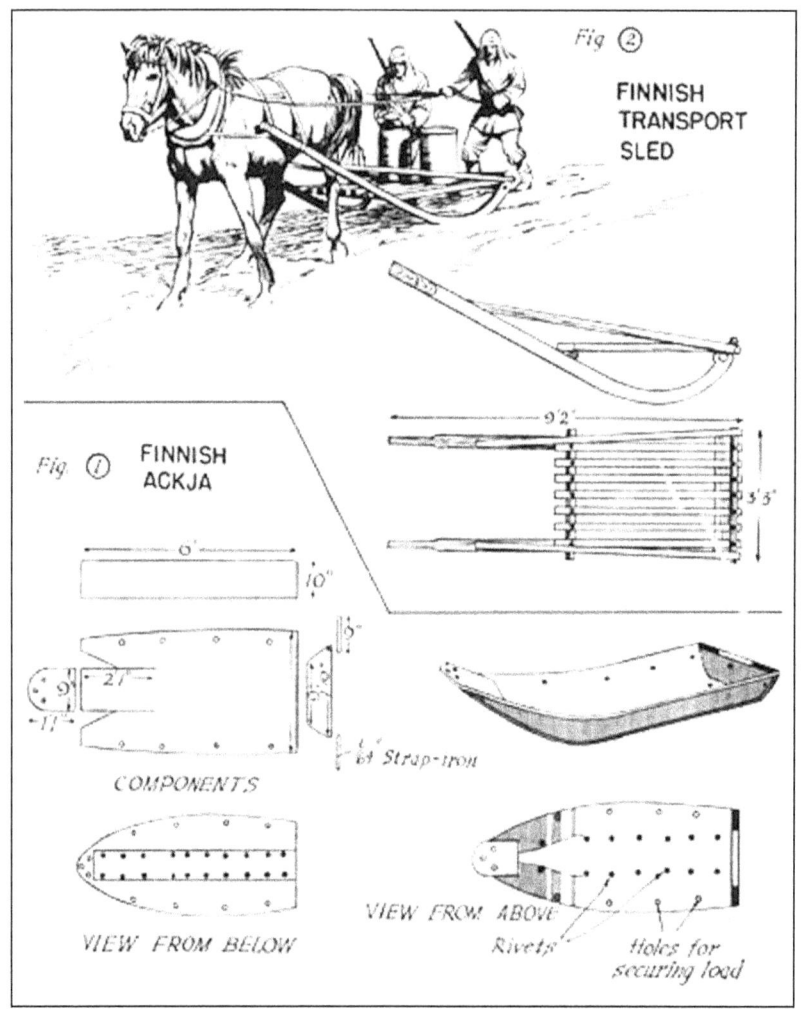

(2) CLINKER-BUILT TYPE
These are stronger but also considerably heavier than the plywood type. They are constructed exactly like a small boat, and move on a single broad runner along the keel.

b. Propulsion
Ackjas can be pulled in two ways:
(1) By Dogs
The normal team is of two dogs, the first being led. Dogs must be specially trained for this work.

(2) By Men on Skis

In deep snow, a team of men commonly go ahead to clear a track of sufficient width to accommodate the sleds.

c. Light Snow Drag

A simple horse-drawn drag, suitable for transport of light loads, is shown in figure 2 of the sketch.

GERMAN AMBULANCE SLED

Tactical and Technical Trends, No. 14, December 17th, 1942.

The evacuation of battlefield casualties over rough country always presents a major logistical problem. This is particularly true where evacuation must be made through deep snow; one solution to the problem of snow may be indicated in a photograph from a German newspaper showing a small snow-sled, evidently for use as an ambulance. It is equipped with three runners, one forward and two in the rear. It is powered by a small 7-cylinder radial airplane engine mounted on the back. The propeller is 2-bladed and made of wood. The propeller guard consists of what appears to be a tubular steel frame protecting only the lower half of the propeller's arc. The sled would probably carry a driver and two patients.

SNOW CAMOUFLAGE

From Camouflage of Vehicles, FM5-20B

From the air, snow-covered terrain is seldom entirely white, but is broken by dark areas of woods, scrub growth, and shadows made by irregularities in the ground surface, such as rock outcrops, ridges, and drainage lines.

Concealment of tracks is a major problem in snow-covered terrain, as unconcealed tracks point the way to concealed installations. In even light snow, tracks make strong shadow lines, visible from a long distance. Sharp turns by vehicles should be avoided because ridges of snow cast heavy shadows. Whenever possible, vehicles should follow shadow-casting terrain lines, staying on the side where shadows are constant throughout the day. It is important that all vehicles keep to the same tracks. Vehicles leaving a road may achieve a short period of track concealment by driving into or away from the sun. Shadows cast by these tracks will not be apparent until the sun strikes them from an angle. Short lengths of tracks which are not too deep may be trampled down with snowshoes.

Parked vehicles painted a solid olive drab can be concealed in snow if there are sufficient natural materials available. Park so shadow of vehicle falls on a bush or on another shadow, and break up shadow pattern of tarpaulin bows with cut foliage. If this is impossible, park facing sun or away from sun to reduce the size of the shadow cast by the vehicle. This shadow may be broken up by piles of snow, by large snow balls, or by holes dug in the snow. Snow thrown on the wheels of a parked vehicle helps to disrupt this tell-tale area.

For vehicles which must operate in areas where snow is a daily problem, concealment is made much easier if they are painted with a snow pattern. Many field-expedient substitutes for paint can be used. Vehicles should be parked close to dark features of the terrain pattern. Concealment by shadows from buildings, ground formations, and trees, though effective in summer, loses much of its usefulness when snow is on the ground, as the white background lightens the shadows of those objects.

Nets are not recommended for draping in snow. They require excessive maintenance, cannot carry a heavy snow load, become wet, bulky, and hard to handle. Garnishing becomes wet, wrinkles, and loses coverage, increasing texture and darkening tone values. They must be removed entirely during snow and sleet storms.

Where nets are used for permanent overhead hammocks or to create permanent parking hides for vehicles, they should be garnished 100 percent. Where the terrain pattern is mottled, as during a thaw period, the perimeter areas of nets should be white; towards the center, apply patterns of slate gray, black, and olive drab. Site nets of this kind near trees, snow drifts, rocks, or other natural forms which cast shadows. Where nets are anchored directly to the ground, heap snow on the edges to relieve the irregularity of outline. All anchor stakes should be of wood. Metal stakes and driftpins conduct heat from the sun and thaw themselves free.

GERMAN WINTER FIELD FORTIFICATIONS AND THE USE OF ICE-CONCRETE

Tactical and Technical Trends, No. 22, April 8th 1943

From the Eastern Front comes a report of the German type of winter field fortifications and shelters, with a description of an effective concrete made of a frozen sand, or sand with broken stone, and water mixture.

a. General

Construction of field fortifications in winter presents a number of special difficulties due to cold, frozen ground, ice, and snow which may occasionally reach a depth of several meters. The men's capacity for work is moreover lowered by extreme cold. For this reason allowance must be made for a considerable increase in time and personnel requirements, often amounting to many times the normal. Special tools and equipment suitable for work under winter conditions must be obtained well in advance.

The depth to which ground is frozen on the Eastern Front often reaches 1.5 meters (5 ft.).

b. Camouflage

In snow-covered terrain, special attention should be paid to concealment against ground and air observation. Paths caused by trampling, ditches, working sites, etc., can be recognized from the air with particular ease. For this reason, before beginning work snow should be cleared to one side so that it may be available for subsequent camouflage, and finished work must again be covered with snow. Trenches can be covered with planks, beams, pine branches, or sheet-iron, on which snow should be heaped.

c. Construction of Shelters, Trenches, and Breastworks

(1) CONSTRUCTION OF EARTH SHELTERS IN FROZEN GROUND

(a) In the presence of the enemy, for speedy and silent preparation of shelters in frozen ground, sandbags are used; for this purpose, canvas rather than paper sacks are to be recommended. Sandbags are filled in the rear, and carried forward to the point where they are to be used. Freezing sandbags by pouring water on them improves their protective properties for the duration of cold weather.

(b) Where the tactical situation permits unimpeded work, the following practice is adopted. In constructing trenches in ground which is not frozen to a great depth, in order to avoid the labor of digging through the frozen ground, the surface is divided up by furrows into the desired sections. These sections are then undermined, and the frozen crust is caved in and removed. For this work heavy pickaxes, crowbars, iron wedges, etc., are necessary.

Deeply frozen ground can be broken up by engineers using power drilling equipment (concrete breakers driven by portable compressors) and explosives. Holes for explosives can be made in frozen ground by driving in red-hot, pointed iron rods or crowbars. In excavating trenches in deeply frozen ground, the best method is to dig holes at an interval of several feet down to the full depth of the trench; these holes are subsequently connected by tunnels under the frozen surface, and finally the surface is caved in.

(2) CONSTRUCTION OF SHELTERS IN SNOW AND EARTH

If the depth of snow is great, fieldworks must be constructed partly in snow and partly in the ground. Small shafts are sunk to the full depth planned and are then connected by trenches dug

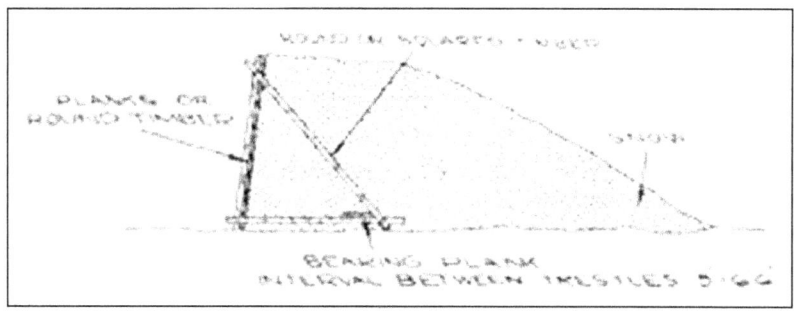

Figure 1

in the snow. The deepening of these trenches into the ground can be carried out later. If there has been only a short frost before the snowfall, the ground will be found to be only slightly frozen, since the snow acts as a protective layer against hard freezing.

(3) CONSTRUCTION OF SHELTERS IN SNOW

If heavy snowfall is to be expected, or if time is short, or if equipment for excavation of frozen ground is not available, breastworks of snow can be erected on the surface. Snow, if it is to be used as protection against enemy fire, must be tamped solid. It must also be camouflaged by scattering loose snow over it. Its effectiveness as a protection is raised by pouring water over it. The rear side of the breastwork should be revetted with sandbags filled with snow; canvas rather than paper should be used for this purpose. Alternative materials are round timber, wire netting, or wooden planks secured to posts, like a fence.

If it is impossible to drive in or anchor the posts, simple trestles of triangular cross section should be erected at intervals of 5 to 6 1/2 feet, as shown in figure 1. The best practice is to carry the trestles ready-made to the site where they are to be used. After adding the revetment and bearing planks, snow is shoveled over it and tamped hard. The center of the snow wall can be formed of any other suitable material: e.g., round timber, stones, gravel, sand, etc.

(4) PROTECTIVE QUALITIES OF SNOW AND ICE

The following are the thicknesses of snow and ice which afford

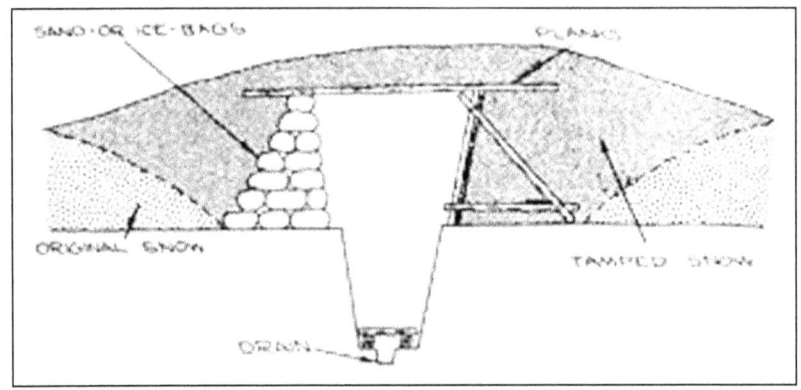

Figure 2

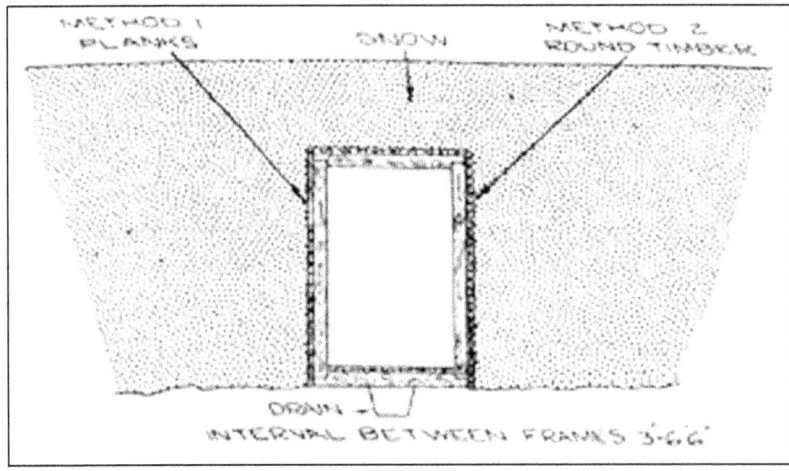

Figure 3

protection against ordinary rifle fire, but NOT against fire concentrated on a single point:

New snow - (minimum) 13 ft

Tamped snow - (minimum) 8 - 10 ft

Frozen snow - (minimum) 6 ft 6 in

Ice - (minimum) 3 ft 3 in

(5) COVERED TRENCHES

Trenches can be covered over to protect them from snowing-up, and to conceal them, as shown in figure 2. The cover of round timbers, sawn timbers, planks, or beams must be strong enough to carry the maximum weight of snow that can be expected.

d. Tunneling in Snow

If the snow is sufficiently deep, tunnels can easily be constructed. They do not provide effective protection against artillery fire, but this disadvantage is considerably outweighed by the complete concealment they afford. The method of construction varies according to the condition of the snow, which may be new (powdery), already frozen, and of varying depths. The following are the methods employed:

(1) Digging in from the surface and covering over with planks and layers of snow;

(2) Digging in from the surface and the construction of sheeting or revetting with planks, beams, brushwood, or sheet-iron;

(3) Underground tunnelling, construction of wooden sheeting or revetting with planks, beams, or brushwood (figure 3);

(4) The construction of tunnels without sheeting (figure 4). In long tunnels, ventilation must be provided by ventilation shafts, as shown in figure 5.

e. Construction of Shelters, Covered Positions, Positions for AT or Infantry Guns, and Ammunition or Supply Shelters

The same methods are used as in construction in the ground. The floor and walls should be constructed with particular care, and the roofing formed of planks or beams. In addition, roofs and walls must be covered with roofing felt, which should also be laid under the floor. Inner insulation must also be provided by mats and straw, layers of wool, or sacking, and cracks should be

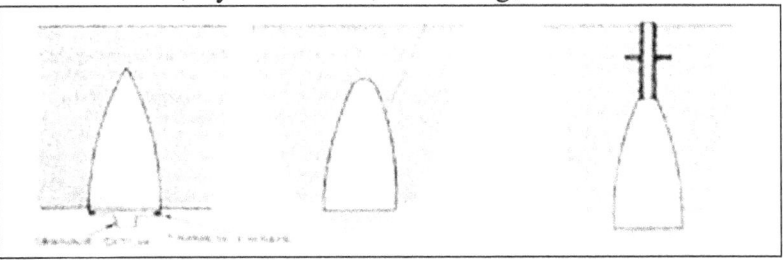

Figure 4 *Figure 5*

filled with moss, sod, or straw. Another effective method of building walls is to use a double revetment of planks with a heat-insulating space between them. The revetment of intermediate space is necessary not only as protection against cold, but also to avoid the melting of the snow by internal heating stoves, etc. Doors and entrances should be small and well fitting. Even if shelters are unheated, a snow covering of sufficient thickness will raise the temperature in shelters of this kind to 3 to 5° C (37 to 41° F). Owing to their slight insulating properties, sheet-iron side walls are suitable only for excavations which are not to be occupied by personnel.

f. Drainage

When a thaw sets in, special provision must be made for draining away water, and this should be provided, when the position is first constructed, by ditches and other methods. Crawl-trenches and tunnels must be built with a gradient sufficient to drain the water away. Failure to observe these precautions will quickly result in the flooding of the excavation and the caving-in of the weakened and undercut walls.

g. "Ice-Concrete"

(1) DEFINITION

Ice-concrete is a dense, frozen mixture of sand and water, or sand with gravel or broken stone and water.

(2) APPLICATION

Ice-concrete is especially suitable for reinforcement of breastworks and for the construction of roofs and shelters. An example is shown in figure 6 on the following page. Ice-concrete can be protected for a considerable period against effects of rising temperature by being covered with earth.

(3) STRENGTH AND COMPOSITION

Ice-concrete is many times stronger than normal ice. Regarding its composition, experience is as follows:

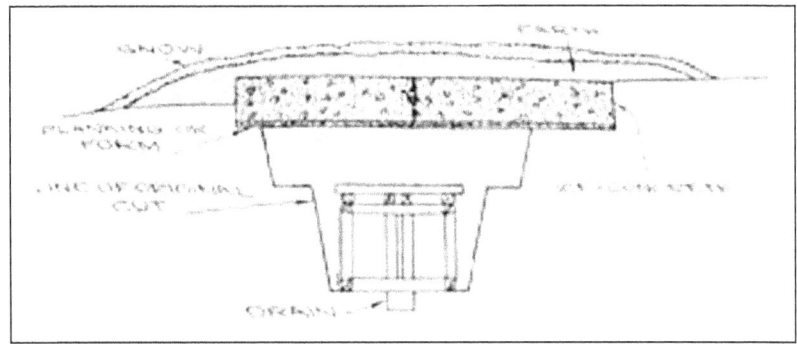

Figure 6

(a) A high proportion of fine sand increases the strength. The strongest mixture of all is composed of sand alone.

(b) If insufficient sand is available, gravel or broken stone can be used. The proportion of fine sand should, however, not fall below 10 percent.

(c) A small proportion of topsoil, clay, or mud is not injurious.

(d) Only as much water should be added as the mixture is capable of absorbing, and as will cause it to become slightly liquid.

(4) PREPARATION OF ICE-CONCRETE

(a) In preparing the mixture by hand, it is shovelled over, if possible in a trough, and the water added gradually; or, mixing can be done in a concrete mixer. The wet mixture is immediately poured into the forms. This operation is carried out in layers of from 4 to 6 inches, accompanied by tamping, in order to consolidate the mixture.

If gravel is used, the material is pre-mixed without adding water. The mixture is then poured into the forms in layers 4 to 6 inches thick, and water is poured in to complete saturation, accompanied by stirring and tamping.

(b) In both cases successive layers should be added as soon as the previous layer is beginning to freeze. Freezing takes place more slowly if the water is added later. In order to hasten the process of freezing, sand and gravel should be already at a freezing temperature before water is added, and the water itself should be as cold as possible. If the material is frozen in large lumps, it should be broken up before mixing.

(c) Ordinary wooden forms should be used, but snow, ice, earth, straw, or brushwood can also be used for this purpose.

As a protection against warming from inside (i.e., heating by stoves, etc.), the inner forms are left standing. The outer forms should be removed as soon as possible in order to hasten freezing.

As a guide, it may be noted that a sheet of ice-concrete, 4 inches thick, will be completely frozen at a temperature of 13 degrees below zero, F°, in 4 to 6 hours.

WINTER FIGHTING IN RUSSIA

*Tactical and Technical Trends,
No. 12, November 19th, 1942.*

The following article has been drawn from Russian sources and gives some information on certain aspects of winter fighting in Russia, but it should be remembered that this article refers to only one sector and that some of the comments concerning tactics as well as equipment might not hold true for other sectors of the front.

In the Mozhaisk area, around which the fighting described below took place, snow was lying about 3 feet deep in the open, and slightly more in the forest. The weather was very cold, with temperatures sometimes reaching -40 degrees Centigrade (-40 degrees Fahrenheit).

The ice on the Dnieper river near Vyazma and on the Moskva river near Mozhaisk, was thick enough to hold light tanks and artillery. Even heavy tanks could cross by using wide wooden tracks laid on the ice.

Because of the deep snow, infantry were able to move off roads and trails only with difficulty, medium and heavy tanks were barely able to get across country, and cavalry and artillery were confined to the immediate proximity of roads and tracks. Operations were consequently tied to existing communications, and very narrow frontages were employed.

Roads had to be constantly cleared of snow, and even parts of the broad Moscow-Minsk highway could be kept cleared only enough to permit two-way traffic.

Under such conditions, the Russians use some special ski troops, but these were not attached to every unit, and certain divisions operating in the Mozhaisk sector did not have them. Part of each infantry regiment, as well as the division motorized company, however, were trained to operate on skis.

A Panzer IV in Russia, September 1943

The German organization included one trained ski company in each battalion and one platoon in every other company. This system was apparently not put into practice, for German skiers were few and poorly trained.

Since many Russians are accustomed to skiing before they are called up, 14 days are allowed for training the normal infantry soldier to operate on skis. The specialist ski troops are given a course of 2 months.

It is reported that during their initial advance the Germans employed a great number of motorcycles. During the winter operations, these were no longer in evidence, although great use was made of bicycles.

The Russian Fifth Army in this sector was operating astride the Mozhaisk-Smolensk road, on a front of about 35 miles, and its normal disposition was with six divisions forward and four in reserve. The division astride the main road worked on a frontage of about 3 1/2 miles, and the normal battalion frontage was about 1,100 yards. Since the advance was normally made along the roads and tracks, actual contact was usually on a very narrow front.

In general, the Russians sought to pin down the enemy garrison by fire, while their main infantry force came forward to finish off the defenders.

They always attempted to gain complete surprise when using these tactics, one of their objects being to deny the Germans time to set fire to buildings. Since surprise was considered so essential, ski parties were rarely accompanied by armored vehicles.

The ski parties were always well-supplied with Tommy guns, and frequently with machine guns and light mortars.

The heavy and medium mortars and antitank guns, pulled on small sleds, were also used. At a later stage medium or heavy tanks were sometimes brought up, either to help forward the main infantry attack or to extricate ski parties which had got into difficulties.

Although the Russians carried out frequent operations by night, the Germans, possibly because they previously had heavy casualties among personnel especially trained for night operations, did not seem to display so much interest in this type of fighting. In the early stages of the war the German troops, including armored units, had made extensive use of night attacks.

At one time during the operations in this sector, the whole of a Russian division's artillery was deployed within 200 or 300 yards of a road, some guns actually firing from the road in column. Although this deployment provided an excellent air target, German air activity was almost negligible, and the Russians could thus afford to take risks.

Russian artillery communications, both wire and radio, were reported good. They used excellent 1/25,000 maps which had enemy positions overlaid by Army Headquarters.

It was found that even deep snow does not lead to more "duds" than under normal conditions. Snow does, however, greatly decrease the fragmentation of shell fire.

In good light the observation of shell fire is much easier in snow-covered country than under normal, summer conditions, but if the light is bad, observation becomes very difficult. For observation, the Russians used a shell with a red smoke-box, experience having shown red to be the most effective color under snow conditions.

In the area between Mozhaisk and Gzatck, the forward German defenses were about 6 miles in front of their main line of resistance. All towns and villages were held as strongpoints, and where villages were some distance apart, they were joined by small defense areas established on roads and paths. These defense areas, however, tended to be rather disconnected and patchy except for the area close to the main line of resistance.

The German strongpoints were generally based on small posts which were designed to take one antitank or machine gun, and which were sited on commanding ground, in groups of four or eight, each post being connected to the other by snow parapet tracks. When time permitted, each post was dug down to a depth of about 4 feet, with a snow and earth parapet, and the whole roofed by logs and boards.

The Russian field defenses, on the other hand, were started with a snow parapet about 8 feet thick. Water was poured on this until it froze, making it bulletproof. If available, logs were used to strengthen it.

For later development, digging was nearly always possible where there was sandy soil. Other types of ground were loosened by charges exploded at a depth of about 4 feet.

The Germans and Russians both used a great deal of heavy wire in forests, with entanglements stretched from tree to tree. Though the German belts of wire sometimes proved a considerable obstacle, it was often found that they were not adequately covered by fire.

In open country the Russians used concertina wire, anchoring it about half embedded in the snow. Frequently they put it completely under the snow in order to obtain surprise, but the latter method, of course, was not used against skiers,

Russian antitank obstacles normally consisted of ditches, wooden posts of at least 6 inches diameter sunk at about 45 degrees, or crow's-feet of very heavy angle-iron. They also used a heavy, coiled, barbed concertina-type wire, buried under the snow to tangle tank tracks. The only effect of snow on antitank obstacles was to make them more difficult to locate and, therefore, more likely to trap a tank.

The Russians found that antitank guns can usually obtain excellent targets if they are sited to fire over areas covered by deep snow, which cuts the speed and maneuvering ability of tanks considerably.

Russian antitank mines were laid at any depth in the snow without their efficiency being affected. As a matter of fact, the more time the Russians had to prepare a minefield, the deeper they put the mines. Both Russians and Germans used a system by which their antitank mines under the snow were linked together in groups for sympathetic explosion.

The Germans soon developed a wooden mine, both for antitank and antipersonnel use, and this mine succeeded, to a large extent, in defeating the efficient Russian mine detector. Neither the Russians nor Germans appear to have made any use of dummy antitank mines.

The Germans used white, red, and green Very lights for signals, but the Russians generally managed to discover their meanings and gain valuable information.

In withdrawal, the Germans sited their defenses in considerable depth and used leapfrog methods of retirement. Each German division normally had a rear guard of an infantry combat team. Divisions usually withdrew on a front of about 6 miles.

The Germans followed a definite policy of destroying all buildings in villages which they evacuated, principally in order to deprive the Russians of accommodations. Destruction proved comparatively easy, since the buildings are normally made of wood.

There was one German armored division in this sector, and the unarmored portion of this unit was detached and used to hold a section of the line. The tanks which were deployed along the front in small groups of four to six were often supported by antitank guns. These groups stuck almost exclusively to roads and trails. The German system, when fighting a rearguard action, seemed to be to present the boldest possible front to the enemy by retaining these small groups on roads leading into the position, keeping them parallel to the new main line of resistance. At the same time they always endeavored to clear at least one lateral track immediately in rear of their main line of resistance, in order to facilitate reinforcement of threatened sections of the line.

German artillery was not very much in evidence in the Mozhaisk sector, and there were few guns heavier than field artillery. The Germans relied mainly on mortars, infantry guns, and antitank guns.

In their main defensive positions the Germans sited their mortars in batteries of four or more, about 500 to 600 yards in the rear of their main line of resistance. Field artillery was sited in depth, although the forward batteries were usually not more than 1,600 or 1,700 yards back. Their normal reaction to any threat was intense fire from the 81-mm mortars, for which they seemed to have a more than adequate supply of ammunition. The Germans usually fired off everything available just before a withdrawal, and the Russians learned that when sudden and very heavy mortar fire came down, and no counterattack materialized, the Germans were almost certainly withdrawing. They were then able to take appropriate action.

In forest country the Germans made every effort to block tracks by felling trees and erecting abatis. Wire was used only

Panzer men in winter coats, Russian Front, January 1944

on those positions which were to be defended for some time.

The Germans destroyed all bridges, both large and small, in their retirement. East of Vyazma they destroyed the railway very effectively, demolishing or removing all sections which the Russians had not already removed in their own retirement. It is of interest to note, however, that despite the destruction, the Russians got a locomotive through to Mozhaisk 7 days after the capture of the town.

The Germans used a large number of antitank and

antipersonnel mines in their retirement, sowing them around demolished bridges or culverts in order to catch vehicles using detours. Some minefields were laid in great depth and entirely filled the clearing normally found at each side of main roads through the forest. They also used delayed-action mines and booby traps, although not to a very great extent. Booby traps were usually attached to bright objects like scissors, spoons, or badges.

Cooperation between small bodies of Russian infantry and their tanks appeared excellent. The infantry's sole method of communication with tanks was by light signals, and these were generally used to indicate a target or an objective to be attacked.

There were very few instances in this sector of German tanks attacking under cover of smoke. When smoke was used, it was apparently put down by a normal Nebelwerfer unit.

The reconnaissance unit of the 5th German Tank Division included a certain number of French Panhard armored cars. These vehicles have completely French armament, including coaxial antitank guns and machine gun, and are equipped with Michelin (heavy pneumatic) tires.

German guns on self-propelled mountings were encountered, but the Russians say that in this sector they were normally employed in a defensive role only.

In the earlier stages of the fighting the Germans were operating fairly actively with flights of three or four planes, but after winter came, their efforts were limited mainly to hit-and-run bombing raids by single machines, and during the Mozhaisk operations the Russians definitely had superiority in the air. Russian air units supporting the army work directly under the control of the army staff, for the Russians have no corps organization. There is an air force staff officer at each divisional headquarters. The Russians claim that any request for air support from the commander of an infantry regiment will be answered by bombs on the ground within 1 hour, provided that aircraft are available.

Russian air support during the Mozhaisk operations consisted chiefly of bombing retreating German columns, taking full advantage of the extent to which the Germans were tied to the roads. In attacks against these columns, Russian aircraft armed with cannon soon found it advantageous to carry antitank projectiles. The importance of adequate antiaircraft fire arrangements for such withdrawing columns needs no emphasis; and the Russians were greatly impressed by the intensity of the fire from German mobile antiaircraft weapons and especially by the volume and control of small-arms fire.

German air attacks against Russian land forces, especially on roads, very often consisted of dive-bombing with 100-kilogram (220-pound) and sometimes, 250-kilogram (550-pound) bombs. The accuracy of the German attacks, however, varied directly with the amount of antiaircraft fire encountered.

For camouflage, Russian specialist ski troops wore white coats with attached hoods, while ordinary infantry not equipped with them usually rolled in the snow before going into action. This makeshift arrangement, which produced a mottled effect, was found especially good against a forest background. Similarly, the best form of vehicle camouflage proved to be a pattern of small blobs of white paint, laid on very thickly.

Against winter air observation it proved practically impossible to conceal work actually in progress. Tracks in snow also presented great difficulties, as did smoke from fires. Against ground observation the judicious piling up of snow was found effective, but white material was needed to conceal loopholes.

The Russians lubricated all their weapons with oil of a specially thin arctic type, and recoil mechanisms were also filled with a special liquid. Water-cooled jackets of machine guns were filled with glycerin. All lubricants used were said to be proof down to at least -50 degrees Centigrade (-58 degrees Fahrenheit). Small arms which gummed up were first wiped entirely dry, lubricated with kerosene, and then fired, before receiving normal lubrication.

Since motor transport of all types gummed up very quickly at low temperatures, the Russians provided heaters for all their vehicles. A 1 1/2-ton truck, for example, would get 1 heater; a heavy tank, 12. In addition, mobile heaters, such as those used for ungumming airplane engines at airdromes, were sometimes used.

The lighter Russian weapons were frequently carried on small sleds consisting of a superstructure on a pair of skis, while heavier sleds, for larger weapons, were often pulled along the narrow forest trails by four ponies harnessed in tandem. Also, about 50 percent of the German transport were reported to be working with sleds.

The Germans' red tracer bullets proved very effective against the snow background; the Russians, except for their antiaircraft, had only white tracer.

The Russians gave troops operating in cold weather one hot meal around dawn and another after nightfall. During the day, however, troops existed on a field ration composed largely of bread. Food for the hot meal was cooked in field kitchens--small trailers on two wheels, several of which were towed behind one truck. The food was then sent forward on sleds, in small metal vacuum-flask containers.

As the Germans withdrew, they often burned the villages behind them, leaving the ground thawed around each house. The Russians at once dug this ground down to about 5 or 6 feet. It was then roofed over with logs, tarpaulin, or brushwood, and floored with brushwood, or with straw if available. A stove, with a pipe chimney, was installed in the dugout. These stoves were usually improvised from old oil drums.

Where there were no villages, the Russians would dig the snow in the forest down to ground level, and build up a thick snow wall around an area of 8 feet by 12 or 15 feet. Evergreen fir branches would be used to line the floor and walls, and the compartment would be roofed with more branches, as well as a tarpaulin, if available. Finally the inevitable stove and chimney were added.

For these winter operations, the Russian soldiers were provided with good thick underclothing, of which they frequently wore two sets. Over this was a thick shirt and pullover. Over the pullover went padded trousers and coat, and then an overcoat or the short sheepskin shuba. Headgear consisted of a fur cap, a winter cap, and, frequently, a scarf belonging to the individual soldier. The Russian soldiers wore two pairs of gloves: an inner pair with the first two fingers and thumbs free; and an outer pair of mittens, worn when the use of the trigger finger was not required. No blankets are carried in a Russian division.

On his feet the individual soldier wore the varlenki or felt boot. Socks were not worn under the varlenki, but a piece of cloth, 2 feet by 1 foot 6 inches, was wrapped about the feet and ankles. In deep snow, trousers were worn outside the varlenki and tied round the bottom to prevent snow getting inside the boot.

Russian opinion is that the varlenki is the most satisfactory footwear for snow, and that it has enough wear in it to last through a complete winter. Although it is a felt boot, the wear is less pronounced than might be expected, since the troops can always march on the soft snow by the road. The varlenki has the advantage of drying very quickly in front of a stove, although this is not usually necessary, for in Russia one normally meets a dry type of snow.

Certain specialist ski troops wear a special ski boot, but the ordinary infantry ski in their varlenki.

The Russians claim that they had very few cases of frostbite, and those that did occur were nearly always due to carelessness. The most dangerous areas were found to be the nose and cheek bones, and for troops in short coats, especially skiers, the private parts. Ski troops were issued warm suspensory bandages. Unit commanders issued vaseline or goose fat to their troops to smear on their faces, when low temperatures combined with sharp winds.

The wounded had to be brought in as quickly as possible if they were to escape frostbite. They were collected by regimental stretcher-bearers using low sleds built on two skis.

The Russians claim that the cold had no numbing effect mentally unless the men were tired; that on the contrary it had rather an opposite result, and that troops could go on for long periods of time provided that they were kept on the move, the limiting factor being lack of sleep.

The Russians noticed an obvious drop in the efficiency of German troops when the temperature fell below -20 degrees Centigrade (-4 degrees Fahrenheit). In extreme cold, Germans frequently allowed themselves to be rounded up in houses rather than go outside and face the cold.

The winter clothing of Germans taken prisoner was definitely inadequate. A few wore a second overcoat, but quite frequently they had only their normal clothes. As a result, many suffered from frostbite.

For keeping open the roads in rear of their advancing troops, the Red Army relied almost entirely on large working parties of peasants, who produced excellent results. Snow ploughs were available but apparently were not utilized to any great extent.

On the Mozhaisk front, partisan fighters were very active behind the German lines, and the various guerrilla bands were in close touch with the Red Army commanders. Parties of 40 or so would come through the German lines, receive definite tasks, such as destruction of specific railway bridges, and return through the enemy lines by night. These partisan fighters were armed with rifles and a few Tommy guns and wore civilian clothes. A number of girls were to be found in these bands, which were composed mainly of middle-aged men.

NOTES ON WINTER USE OF INFANTRY WEAPONS

From Intelligence Bulletin, October 1943

1. INTRODUCTION

The following notes are based on directions issued by the German High Command regarding the use of German infantry weapons in winter. For complete descriptions of these weapons, with illustrations, the reader is referred to Special Series No. 14, "German Infantry Weapons," issued by M.I.D., W.D.

2. USE OF INFANTRY WEAPONS IN WINTER

A. GENERAL

The German Army is thoroughly aware that winter cold and snow necessitate special measures concerning the carrying, moving, and bringing into position of infantry weapons and ammunition. In this connection German soldiers are reminded of certain fundamental points: that noises travel farther in cold, clear air; that when snow obscures terrain features, there are decidedly fewer landmarks; and that, in winter, distances are generally estimated too short in clear weather and too far in mist. The German High Command adds several other practical suggestions:

It will be especially necessary to practice target designation, distance estimation, and ranging.

The rifleman and his weapons must be camouflaged thoroughly. White coats, white covers for headgear, and white overall trousers and jackets will be worn. When necessary, such outer clothing can easily be improvised out of white canvas. The simplest camouflage for weapons will be plain white cloth covers or coats of removable chalk; the former will have the added advantage of affording protection.

Figure 2.— "Snow Board" Used as a Base for German Light Machine Gun in Firing Position.

At low temperatures, the accompanying weapons of the infantry will fire somewhat short at first. After a few rounds, however, the range to the point of impact will be normal. Before a weapon is loaded, the loading movements should be practiced without ammunition. (In drilling with pistols, be sure to remove the magazine beforehand.)

B. SPECIFIC

(1) Rifles.

Rifles are carried on the back, or are hung from the neck and suspended in front. During long marches on skis, rifles are fastened on the side of the haversack.

When the German soldier goes into position, he takes special care not to allow his rifle barrel to become filled with snow. He does not take off the bolt protector and muzzle cap until shortly before he is to use the rifle. The various methods of going into position are practiced in drill.

As far as possible, telescopic sights are not exposed too suddenly to extreme changes in temperature.

(2) Automatic Pistol.

The Germans keep the automatic pistol well wrapped, and sling it around the neck or over the shoulder. Magazine pouches are closed very tightly.

(3) Light Machine Gun.

The light machine gun is slung on the back. In going into position, the Germans use brushwood or a "snow board" (see fig. 2) for a base. They take care not to disturb, by unnecessary trampling, the snow cover in front of positions. The purpose of this precaution is to avoid recognition by the opposing force.

The simplest kind of mat is taken along so that belts can be kept clear of snow.

The light machine gun is first shot until it is warm, and then is oiled.

When fire is continued for any length of time, the snow in front of the muzzle turns black; therefore, before the snow becomes blackened, the Germans decide upon prospective changes of position.

If there is to be a considerable interval after the firing of the machine gun, the bolt is changed and the oil is removed from the sliding parts. (Only an extremely thin oil film is allowed to remain.) This precludes stoppages which might be caused by the freezing of oil. The new bolt is given a very thin coat of oil before it is inserted.

Replacement ammunition, in pre-filled belts, is carried into action.

(4) Heavy Machine Gun.

The heavy machine gun is carried in the usual manner or is loaded on a small sleigh, skis, or a pulk. A pulk (see fig. 3) is a type of sled used by the Lapps; its front half somewhat resembles that of a rowboat.

When the Germans take the heavy machine gun into position, they use some sort of snow board, the pulk, or even a stretcher

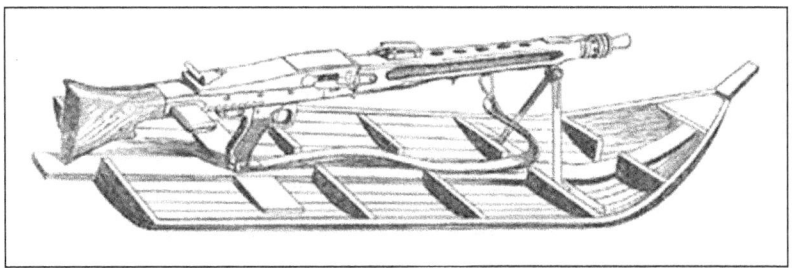

Figure 3.—Pulk Used for Winter Transport of German Heavy Machine Gun.

as a base. They take care not to disturb the snow in front of the position.

The Germans try not to expose the sights to temperatures of less than 6° F. During marches these sights are kept in their containers, and before they are used, they are gradually warmed in sheltered places or on the human body. The sights are kept mounted on the machine-gun carriage only while the gun is in active use.

Mats are carried so that belts may be kept clear of snow.

For shooting in extreme cold, German range tables provide for the necessary sight adjustments. The heavy machine gun is first shot until it is warm, and then is oiled. New positions are decided upon before the snow in front of the muzzle becomes blackened.

The Germans prevent soiling of the machine gun, which leads to stoppages, (a) by keeping the antidust cover closed as much as possible, and (b) by not allowing the gun to remain loaded (with bolt backwards) for any length of time.

Speed is considered highly important in readying the gun for firing. While firing is in progress, the bolt remains uncocked in the forward position, the belt is inserted into the belt pawl, and the gunner, remaining in the firing position, withdraws the cocking slide only with a strong jerk and pushes it forward again.

(5) General Rules for Firing the Mortar and Infantry Howitzers.

Adjustment of fire is done only by very careful bracketing.

At low temperatures, the weapons fire somewhat short at first. After a few rounds the range to the point of impact becomes normal. Therefore, in adjustment of fire, the Germans start with a greater range than that ascertained.

When shooting from the same emplacement for any length of time, the Germans repeatedly throw fresh snow over the black spots in front of the muzzle to camouflage them.

(6) Light Mortar.

The light mortar is carried in the usual manner. In emplacing it, the Germans clear away the snow and dig into the ground. If the snow is loose enough, the Germans fill sandbags with it or pack it down to form bases.

The Germans have found that the fragmentation effect of the mortar shells is diminished by deep snow.

Sights are wrapped in wool as a protection against extreme cold.

(7) Light Infantry Howitzer.

The light infantry howitzer is moved by spur wheel (horse-drawn) or on a simple sleigh, drawn by two horses or six men. When half-tracks or tractors are used, sled runners are placed under the front wheels.

When the ground is frozen solid, the guns in firing position are put on elastic bases whenever this is feasible. Brushwood fascines (bundles) are considered especially satisfactory. When the Germans are firing in deep snow, they use sled runners and snow plates or boards, or the largest commercially-produced snowshoes, to prevent the guns from sinking in. If one pair of snowshoes is not enough, two pairs are fastened together.

Since the march is generally confined to roads or trails, emplacements are usually set up in the route itself.

The Germans try to fire ricochet bursts. This is possible if there is loose snow (up to about 16 inches in depth) and frozen ground.

Sights are protected against extreme cold.

(8) Heavy Infantry Howitzer.

Movement in 6 to 8 inches of snow is not difficult on roads and trails.

For the rest, see (6) and (7).

(9) 37-mm Antitank Gun.

In 6 to 8 inches of snow, the 37-mm antitank gun is drawn by a light five-passenger personnel carrier. When the gun is man-handled or horse-drawn, the Germans use a spur wheel and sled runners fixed underneath.

The emplacement is prepared in the same manner as that of the light infantry howitzer.

The front of the protective shield is painted white. When the gun is in the firing position, a cut-out board is placed underneath the trail.

To avoid blackening the snow with the first round, the weapon is not fired too low over snow cover.

(10) 50-mm Antitank Gun.

In 6 to 8 inches of snow, the 50-mm antitank gun is drawn by a half-track prime mover on roads and trails only.

For the rest, see (9).

RUSSIAN TANK CAMOUFLAGE IN WINTER

Tactical and Technical Trends,
No. 17, January 28th, 1943.

The following report is a translation of a Russian article on tank camouflage in winter. The original article was written by a colonel in the Russian Army.

a. General

Winter camouflage of tanks presents a problem with certain special features, created on the one hand by the general winter background, and on the other by weather conditions which greatly affect the tanks themselves and their employment under combat conditions. In winter the change in the operational characteristics of the tanks and in the conditions of employing them in combat will influence the work to be done toward camouflaging them.

Winter conditions (as has been shown by combat experience) create considerable difficulties for the camouflage of tank units. In winter the principal characteristics of a region are its uniform white background, a lack of outline, and an almost complete absence of color. The only exceptions are small settlements, woods, and thick underbrush. Forests whose dense foliage provides perfect concealment in the summertime lose their masking qualities completely in the winter. In winter, on an even, white blanket of snow, camouflage is very difficult. Almost all methods of camouflage employed in summer prove inapplicable. It is necessary to make wide use of special winter covering for the vehicles, and to paint them with winter paint: all one color (protective coat) or in large spots (disruptive).

In winter, tracks made by moving vehicles can be easily recognized, not only from the air but also from high ground observation posts. The removal of tracks left by tanks is the personal responsibility of the commander of the tank units and of the crews. The presence of a blanket of snow, which is often very thick, greatly reduces the mobility of tanks, and as a result reduces the possibility of tanks appearing quickly and suddenly from directions unexpected by the enemy. Tanks cannot go through more than 3 inches of snow without appreciable loss of speed. The deepest snow through which a tank can go is 3 feet; for practical purposes tanks can operate in 1 1/2 feet of snow. It is apparent that these conditions greatly reduce the possibility of using approach routes concealed from enemy observation. Snow makes it necessary for tanks to employ existing roads, which means that they must engage in all their combat operations in those parts of the terrain which are under the special observation of the enemy.

An important winter factor from the point of view of concealment is the longer period of darkness, which helps to conceal the movement and disposition of tanks, provided, of course, that all camouflage measures are carefully observed.

Another winter factor which may be considered important from the point of view of camouflage and concealment is the greater cloudiness of the sky, which hinders reconnaissance activity by enemy aviation and sometimes stops it completely. Then too, tanks may make use of snowstorms which produce conditions of bad visibility and audibility, and as a result tend to lessen vigilance on the part of enemy observation posts.

b. Tank Painting

In winter, tanks are painted all white when the aim is to avoid observation, and in two colors with large spots when the aim is to avoid identification. As a rule, all-white paint is employed in level, open country characterized by a lack of variegated color. Two-color disruptive winter paint is used where the ground presents a variety of color, where there are forests, underbrush, small settlements, thawed patches of earth, etc.

One-color camouflage paint is applied to all parts of the tank in one or two coats. For the paint, zinc white or tytanium white is used only with an oil base, and slight amounts of ultramarine coloring. For the lack of anything better, the tanks may be painted with chalk dissolved in water.

Painting in two colors with large spots can be undertaken in two ways: one is to paint only part of the tank surface, leaving about 1/4 or 1/3 of the tank's surface in the original green; another is to repaint the tank entirely in two colors, either white and dark gray, or white and gray-brown.

When the weather is cold, painting should take place in a warm place, since paint applied when the temperature is 10° below zero Fahrenheit is too hard to be applied.

In winter, as in summer, it is necessary to avoid mechanical repetition of patterns and colors. For example, in painting the tanks of a platoon, one or two tanks are painted white, a third in white irregular stripes leaving parts of the protective green paint as it is, the fourth with white and dark gray spots, and finally, the fifth with white and grayish-brown spots.

c. Covers and Ground Masks

For winter tank camouflage, one may use nets made of cord which have fastened to them irregular white patches of fabric, about 1 yard across. A large all-white cover also may be used.

When using white winter covers, it is necessary to pay attention to the degree of whiteness of the materials used, for even if a little yellow shows or if part of the material is soiled, it will sharply outline the cover and the tank against the background of pure white snow. A simple method to improve this camouflage is to place a thin layer of snow on the cover.

In winter, ground masks are also used. But the construction of these camouflage masks involves special considerations dependent on the character of the background. The principal camouflage materials employed are irregularly shaped pieces of white fabric or painted white matting. In addition to the white patches, dark patches should be fastened to the material to give the appearance of bushes, tree tops, or other natural ground features. For dark patches one may use tree branches and other similar materials. As with covers, the use of white patches alone, or of a combination of white and dark patches, will depend entirely on the terrain and the coloration of the surroundings.

To attach the patches to the mask, they are frozen on after wetting the material with water.

d. Dummy Tanks

Drawing the attention of the enemy to dummy tanks has the same aim in wintertime as in summer, namely, to deceive the enemy concerning the disposition, types, and character of tank activity. However, in winter the making of dummy tanks is subject to certain special conditions. Large dummy snow tanks may be made by packing snow into the form of a tank, showing the hull, the suspension system, and the turret, and then spraying with paint. Movable life-size models are constructed not on wheels but on skis. "Flat" models may be made simply by treading the snow into the contours of a tank. In all other respects the making and use of dummy tanks in winter is no different than in summer.

e. Camouflage while in Motion

Generally speaking, winter conditions make it necessary to move along existing roads. Since winter roads appear to the aerial observer as dark strips, tanks which have an all-white winter paint stand out fairly clearly. In view of the fact that vehicles can be spotted by the shadow they cast, they should move on the side of the road nearest to the sun so that their shadow falls on the road, which is darker than the snow next to the road. Movement along the roads, especially at great speeds and over fluffy dry snow, gives itself away by clouds of snow dust. For this reason, movement of vehicles in wintertime should be at low speeds, especially over new-fallen snow. The tracks left by the tank treads stand out clearly as two dark parallel strips with tread impressions. These can be obliterated by sweeping the road. When tracks are left on the hard crust of the existing road it is necessary, instead of sweeping, to remove them with the aid of graders.

When the tanks pass through places where turns are unavoidable, there appear everywhere little heaps of upturned snow; these are characteristic marks and betray the movement of tanks. To prevent this, turns must be made gradually in a wide arc whenever practicable, or else the heaps of snow which are formed must be cleared away.

The reflection from the lenses of the tank headlights will also give away their movement. In order to prevent this, it is necessary to cover the headlights with white fabric covers, or some other material.

Finally, among the most important factors betraying the movement of tanks to ground observers is the clank of the tracks. [Russian tanks tracks are of all-metal construction.] The noise of these can be heard better as the temperature falls. Naturally, when operations are in the immediate vicinity of the enemy, one makes use not only of all the ordinary precautions employed in summer for the prevention of noise, but takes into account the special characteristics of winter weather with its increased transmission of sound.

f. Camouflage of Stationary Tanks

In winter, tanks are, generally speaking, parked alongside buildings and in woods and shrubbery; in exceptional cases it may be necessary to station tanks in open flat country or in gullies.

The peculiar characteristic of inhabited areas in wintertime from the point of view of camouflage is the motley appearance of the landscape due to the presence of dwelling places, barns, gardens, roads, and paths. This wealth and variety of outline affords considerable opportunities for concealing the position of tanks from air and ground observation by the enemy.

As a rule, all vehicles in bivouac should be placed under the roofs of sheds and barns. Only where there is an insufficient number of such structures, or where the size of the vehicles makes it impossible to place the vehicles in the existing shelters, is it necessary to build shelters, resembling the existing structures in the given locality. The roofs of these shelters must be covered with a layer of snow so that they will not look any different from the roofs of the existing structures. Just as in summertime, these camouflage structures may be built either as additions to existing structures or as separate structures. The separate camouflage structures should be situated along laid-out paths, and the tracks of the caterpillars which lead to the place where the tanks are stationed should be swept or dragged so as to resemble an ordinary road.

When there is not enough time to construct shelters, it is sometimes possible (as on the outskirts of a village) to camouflage tanks by simulating haystacks, piles of brushwood, stacks of building materials, etc. This is done by strewing over the vehicle a certain quantity of material at hand and covering it with a thin layer of snow.

Woods, orchards, and brushwood can be used for camouflage purposes in the wintertime only if additional camouflage precautions are taken. Since leafy woods offer much less concealment in winter than in summer and do not hide the vehicles from air observation, they must be covered with white covers, and there should be strewn over them broken branches or some other camouflage material such as hay, straw, etc.

When there are no white covers, the vehicles may be covered with dark ones, but snow must be placed on top and scattered. Dark covers can be used only against a background which has natural black spots. Finally, if no covers of any kind are available, the vehicles should be covered with branches, straw, hay, and the like, and snow placed on top in irregular patches.

When the tanks are stationed in open flat country, then the camouflage of the tanks also involves the breaking up of the uniform aspect of the locality, which is done by treading around on the snow. Then these areas are given irregular form by scattering here and there patches of pine needles, straw, and rubbish. The ground should also be laid bare, as tanks which are painted a dark color will not be easily discovered against a dark background, either by visual air observation or by the study of aerial photographs.

In open country, thaws are particularly favorable to camouflage of tanks, for the disappearing snow exposes portions of the surface of the ground. The result is that the ground assumes a naturally mottled appearance, and the contours of vehicles stationed there are easily blended. When there is deep snow, tanks may be placed in snow niches built near snowdrifts along the road. The entrances to these should be directly off the road in order to avoid tell-tale tracks of the treads. On the top the niches are covered with white covers, or with some other available material over which snow is placed. In order to camouflage the entrance, it is necessary to use hangings of white cloth or painted mats which may be readily let down or pulled up.

When the tank is stationed in a gully, it is covered with solid white covers of any kind of fabric or matting painted white, or by the regulation net, with white and black patches attached to it.

ENGINEER PRACTICES IN WINTER

*From Tactical and Technical Trends,
No. 36, October 21st, 1943.*

a. General

A German engineering training manual contains the following account of the preparation of obstacles, minefields and demolitions under winter conditions. The depths of snow in which mines become unreliable is of particular interest in view of the number of unverified reports that mines will detonate when deeply buried. The load distribution (i.e., the spreading out of the load over a greater area as the depth below the surface increases) through snow from wheeled and in particular, semi-tracked vehicles is, no doubt, appreciable. There must, therefore be a limiting depth at which a given mine may be set and still function under the desired surface load.

Thus far, there has been no evidence of electrified fences on the Russian front, but there have been unconfirmed reports of their use in western Europe.

The possibility of erecting obstacles is greatly affected by winter conditions. Deep snow forms in itself a natural obstacle; it hinders troop movements on roads and across country. Under conditions of deep snow, movement is in general limited to roads and paths which have been previously tracked, or from which the snow has been removed. For this reason particular significance is attached to obstacles on roads. Tank movements are delayed by deep snow. According to present experience, tanks can force a passage through snow up to a depth of two feet; but snow considerably reduces their capacity for climbing.

b. Natural Obstacles

Natural obstacles in winter are considerably more effective than under normal conditions. Frozen rivers can be transformed into obstacles by demolition of the ice-covering. As obstacles they will remain effective for a length of time depending on the rate of flow and on the temperature, also on the possibility of keeping them open in the face of enemy action. Slowly moving rivers and lakes cannot be kept open. The method of demolishing the ice-cover is to blow holes in it; through these holes the main demolition charges are placed under the ice by means of poles. The effectiveness of steep banks and excavations as good antitank obstacles is increased by deep snow.

c. Artificial Obstacles

The following are artificial obstacles: wire fences, wire snares, trip wires and barbed wire rolls.

(1) WIRE OBSTACLES

(a) Erection in frozen ground. In frozen ground iron pickets, which can be hammered in, are more practicable than wooden pickets. Sockets for pickets can be prepared by engineers using power drilling equipment and demolition charges.

(b) Erection of wire obstacles in anticipation of deep snow. If deep snow conditions are to be expected, specially long pickets must be used in erecting wire obstacles. Wire can easily be set at the necessary height in woods and forests by attaching it to trees. If time is lacking, or there is uncertainty as to whether snowfall will occur, the upper strands of wire can if conditions permit be added later. A specially raised wire fence is illustrated in figure 1 overleaf.

(c) Erection of wire obstacles on frozen snow. On a frozen snow surface pickets can be erected with the aid of heavy nails and cross-timbers, as shown in figure 2 overleaf. Another method of erecting an obstacle on snow is shown in figure 3 overleaf. Obstacles erected on snow have the disadvantage that under certain conditions they may easily sink.

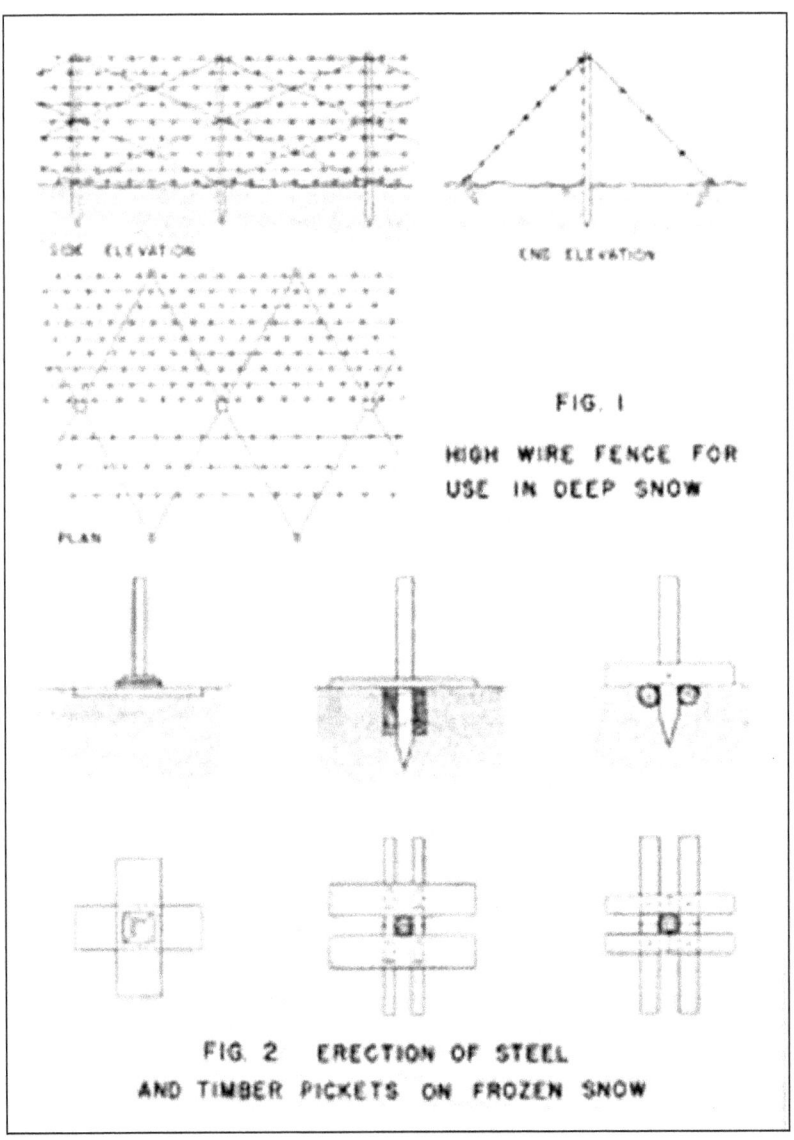

FIG. 1 HIGH WIRE FENCE FOR USE IN DEEP SNOW

FIG. 2 ERECTION OF STEEL AND TIMBER PICKETS ON FROZEN SNOW

(d) Simple warning devices, in the form of empty tin cans containing small stones or nails should be attached to all wire obstacles.

(e) Wire obstacles must be provided, on the side facing the enemy, with chevaux-de-trise, or rolls of plain or barbed wire.

(f) Construction of electrified wire obstacles on ice. Electrified

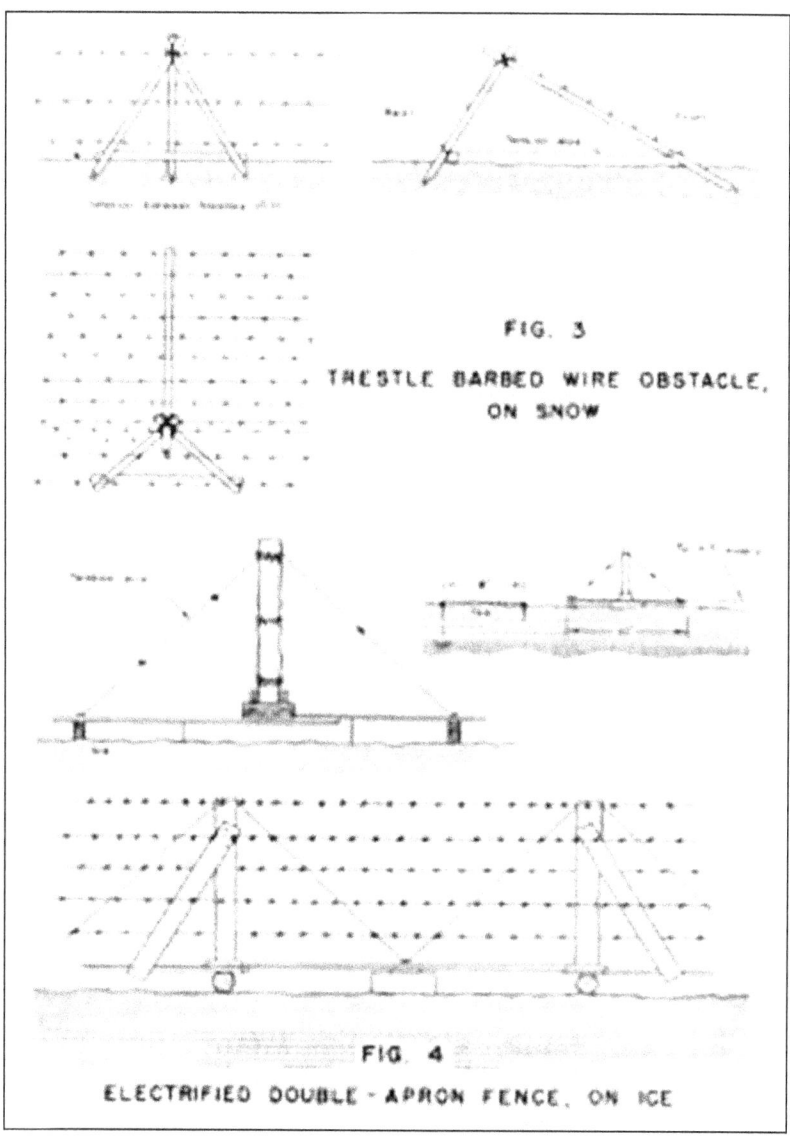

FIG. 3
TRESTLE BARBED WIRE OBSTACLE, ON SNOW

FIG. 4
ELECTRIFIED DOUBLE - APRON FENCE, ON ICE

wire obstacles can only be erected on ice by specially trained personnel. Simple wire fence, rolls of plain or barbed wire and multiple-fence obstacles in the form of several single fences. can all be constructed. Owing to the non-conducting properties of ice, a length of wire netting, eight feet in width, must be laid as a ground one foot in front of the electrified obstacle, and must be well connected to the ice by iron pickets

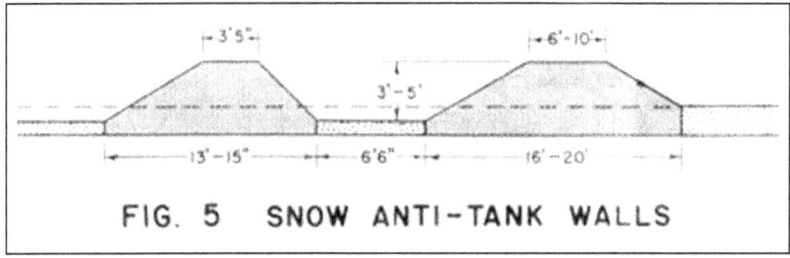

FIG. 5 SNOW ANTI-TANK WALLS

every 30 feet. If possible, the ground should be carried right through to the river bed. Its effect can be increased by heavy snowfall. The obstacle is assembled as shown in figure 4 on the previous page, and erected on the ice.

(2) ANTITANK OBSTACLES
(a) Snow as an obstacle. A continuous snow cover more than 2 feet deep forms a good obstacle against attack by tanks. The exact depth of snow which forms a complete obstacle to attack by tanks is not yet known, and snow should never be completely relied upon as an antitank obstacle.
(b) Construction of snow walls. An effective antitank obstacle is provided by two snow walls built one behind the other, as shown in figure 5. The snow should be lightly tamped down.
(c) Artificial formation of ice. Roads can be made difficult of passage for enemy vehicles, armored cars, etc., by artificial icing. This is specially effective on steep gradients and slopes. Construction of snow walls in combination with the stretch that has been iced increases the effectiveness of the antitank obstacle. Ice-concrete obstacles can also be made

(3) MINEFIELDS
The laying of minefields depends on snow conditions. Under a snow layer of one foot or more, Tellermines are no longer certain of detonation. S-mines (jumping mines) which have already been laid remain effective through frost and thaw, but are not certain of functioning under a depth of snow of four inches or more. Increasing depth of snow diminishes the capacity for

detonation, and at a depth of 10 inches detonation will no longer take place. Mines of any type which have been frozen in should not be lifted, but must be demolished....

D. HANDLING OF DEMOLITION STORES

German explosives are unaffected by cold, and retain their properties through all conditions of weather and storage. In general the following precautions should be observed:

(1) Demolition stores should be kept dry in shelters, separated from each other on wooden supports, and protected from extreme variations in temperature.

(2) Safety fuze, 1930 pattern (Zeitzündschmur 30) must be protected against cold. Safety fuze which has been frozen should be gradually warmed before use, otherwise it is liable to break.

(3) Demolition stores must be examined at frequent intervals; if in bulk, they should not be opened, but the condition of the outer layers only should be tested.

About Coda Books

Most Coda books are edited and endorsed by Emmy Award winning film maker and military historian Bob Carruthers, producer of Discovery Channel's Line of Fire and Weapons of War and BBC's Both Sides of the Line. Long experience and strong editorial control gives the military history enthusiast the ability to buy with confidence.

The series advisor is David McWhinnie, producer of the acclaimed Battlefield series for Discovery Channel. David and Bob have co-produced books and films with a wide variety of the UK's leading historians including Professor John Erickson and Dr David Chandler.

Where possible the books draw on rare primary sources to give the military enthusiast new insights into a fascinating subject.

The English Civil Wars

The Zulu Wars

Into Battle with Napoleon 1812

Waterloo 1815

The Anglo-Saxon Chronicle

The Battle of the Bulge

The Normandy Campaign 1944

Hitler's Justification for WWII

Hitler's Mein Kampf - The Roots of Evil

I Knew Hitler

Mein Kampf - The 1939 Illustrated Edition

The Nuremberg Trials Volume 1

For more information, visit www.codabooks.com

www.ingramcontent.com/pod-product-compliance
Lightning Source LLC
Chambersburg PA
CBHW050903160426
43194CB00011B/2267